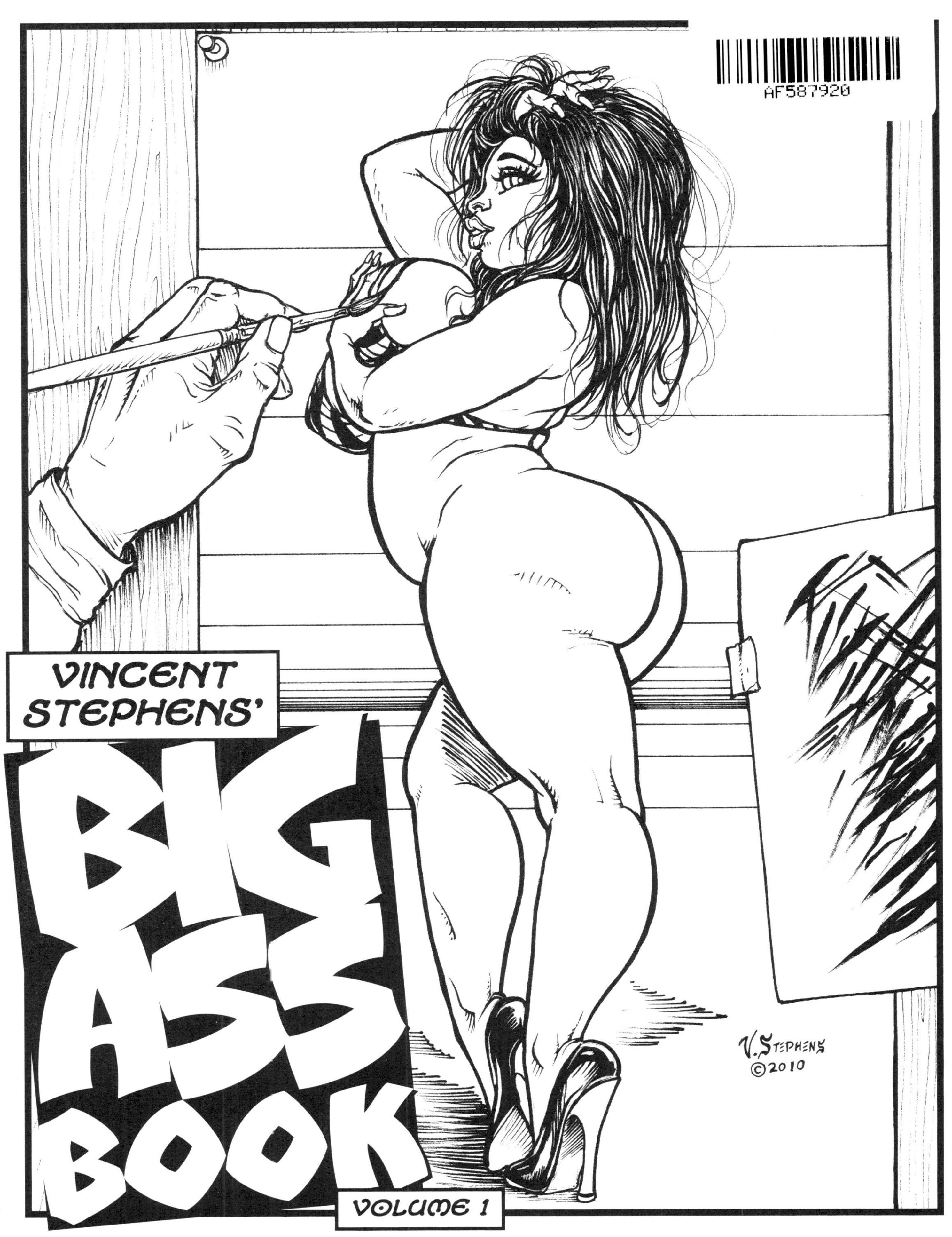
AF587920
VINCENT STEPHENS'
BIG ASS BOOK
VOLUME 1
V. STEPHENS
©2010

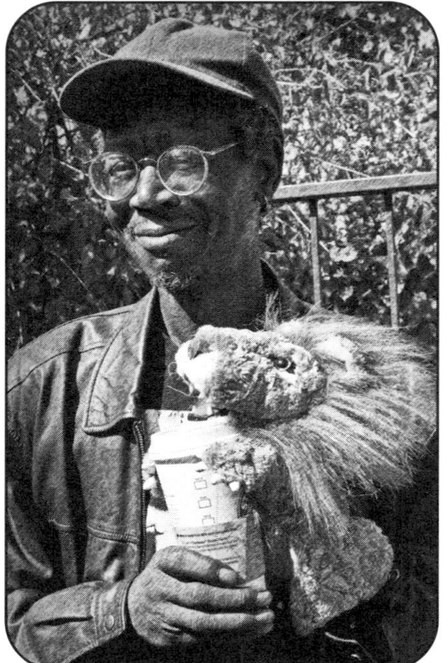

# BUTT I DIGRESS...

## SOME THOUGHTS FROM A GENUINE REAR-ADMIRAL

A LITTLE OVER YEAR AGO I WAS ASKED WHAT I THOUGHT OF THE IDEA OF DOING 'VINCENT STEPHENS' BIG ASS BOOK'. MY RESPONSE, OF COURSE, WAS "HELL YEAH! I LIKE IT!". IN THE FOLLOWING WEEKS AND MONTHS I DEVOTED QUITE A BIT OF THOUGHT TO THE IMPLICATIONS OF PUTTING TOGETHER A COLLECTION OF WORK CELEBRATING THE WONDERFULNESS OF THE BADONKADONK...JUNK IN THE TRUNK...BUNS... CANS...GLUTES...THE BUTT. NOT JUST ANY BUTTS, MIND YOU. I'M TALKING ABOUT AMPLE CURVACEOUS ONE IN ALL THEIR TANTALIZING QUASI-GLOBULAR GLORY. GIVEN THE PROFUSION OF WEBSITES, MAGAZINE, VIDEOS AND SUCH AIMED AT AN "URBAN" DEMOGRAPHIC (THOUGH I PERSONALLY DON'T SEE THE APPEAL BEING LIMITED JUST TO CITY DWELLERS), THIS SAW THIS IS A PROJECT I COULD REALLY GET BEHIND, IF YOU'LL PARDON THE OBVIOUS INTENDED PUN.

ONCE UPON A TIME I WAS CONTENT TO PORTRAY THE STANDARD ISSUE MODEL TYPE. IT'S LEGIT AND THERE ARE TONS OF ARTISTS WHO DO IT MASTERFULLY. AT SOME POINT, PERHAPS OWING TO A SHIFT IN MY OWN THINKING, I STARTED LOOKING AT AND APPRECIATING THOSE WOMEN WHO FELL OUTSIDE THE CONFINES OF WHAT WAS CONSIDERED "IDEAL". TRUTH IS, THERE ARE SOME INCREDIBLY HOTLY SENSUAL WOMEN WHO BRING THE FLAVOR OF THE THICKNESS. AS A PINUP ARTIST I LIKE THE CHALLENGE OF CAPTURING THE FORM, THE SENSE OF VOLUME AND HEFT. I ENJOY TRYING TO CAPTURE THE ATTITUDE AND MOOD THAT MAKES IT MORE THAN JUST ILLUSTRATING A SET OF PHYSICAL ATTRIBUTES. I LIKE DOING WHAT VERY FEW, IF ANY, OTHERS ARE DOING. MORE THAN THE SENSE OF SATISFACTION I DERIVE FROM CREATING THE ARTWORK, IT'S JUST PLAIN FUN TO DO.

AND SO WE HAVE THIS VOLUME. IT IS MY HOPE THAT YOU FIND IT TO YOUR LIKING. I WOULD BE REMISS IF I DID NOT EXPRESS MY GRATITUDE TO SAL AND BOB AT SQP FOR THEIR CONTINUED ENCOURAGEMENT AND SUPPORT. MY THANKS ALSO EXTEND TO JOSE CANO FOR THE KILLER COLOR WORK ON THE COVER ART AND TO YOU FOR YOUR KIND INDULGENCE IN ACQUIRING THIS COLLECTION OF WORKS.

IN CLOSING, I JUST WANT TO PUT OUT THIS LITTLE THOUGHT NUGGET TO PERUSE: THE NEXT TIME A WOMAN MAKES THE INEVITABLE QUERY "DO THESE <INSERT ARTICLE OF CLOTHING HERE> MAKE MY ASS LOOK BIG?", COUNTER WITH "HOW CAN THAT BE A BAD THING? I'M LOVIN' IT."

THEN SHOW HER THIS BOOK.

NOW CUE UP SIR MIX-A-LOT...

VINCENT STEPHENS

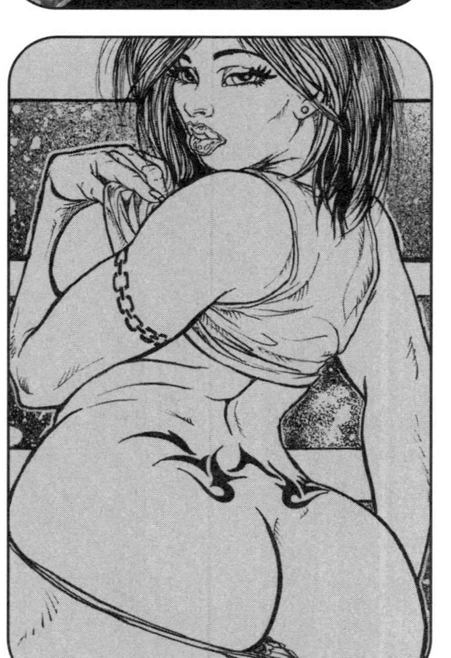

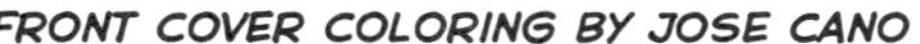

*FRONT COVER COLORING BY JOSE CANO*

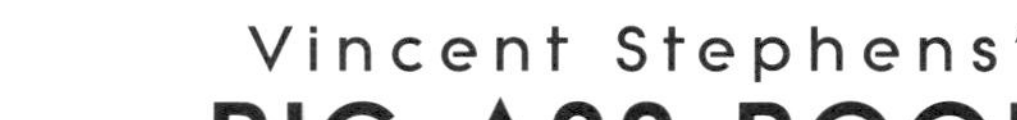

Vincent Stephens'
**BIG ASS BOOK**
Volume One

Book design by Grassy Knoll Studios.

Published by
SQP Inc.
PO Box 248 - Columbus, NJ 08022

Sal Quartuccio & Bob Keenan - Publishers

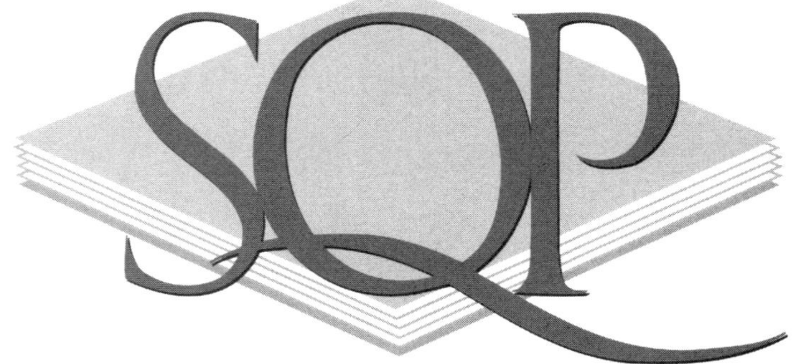

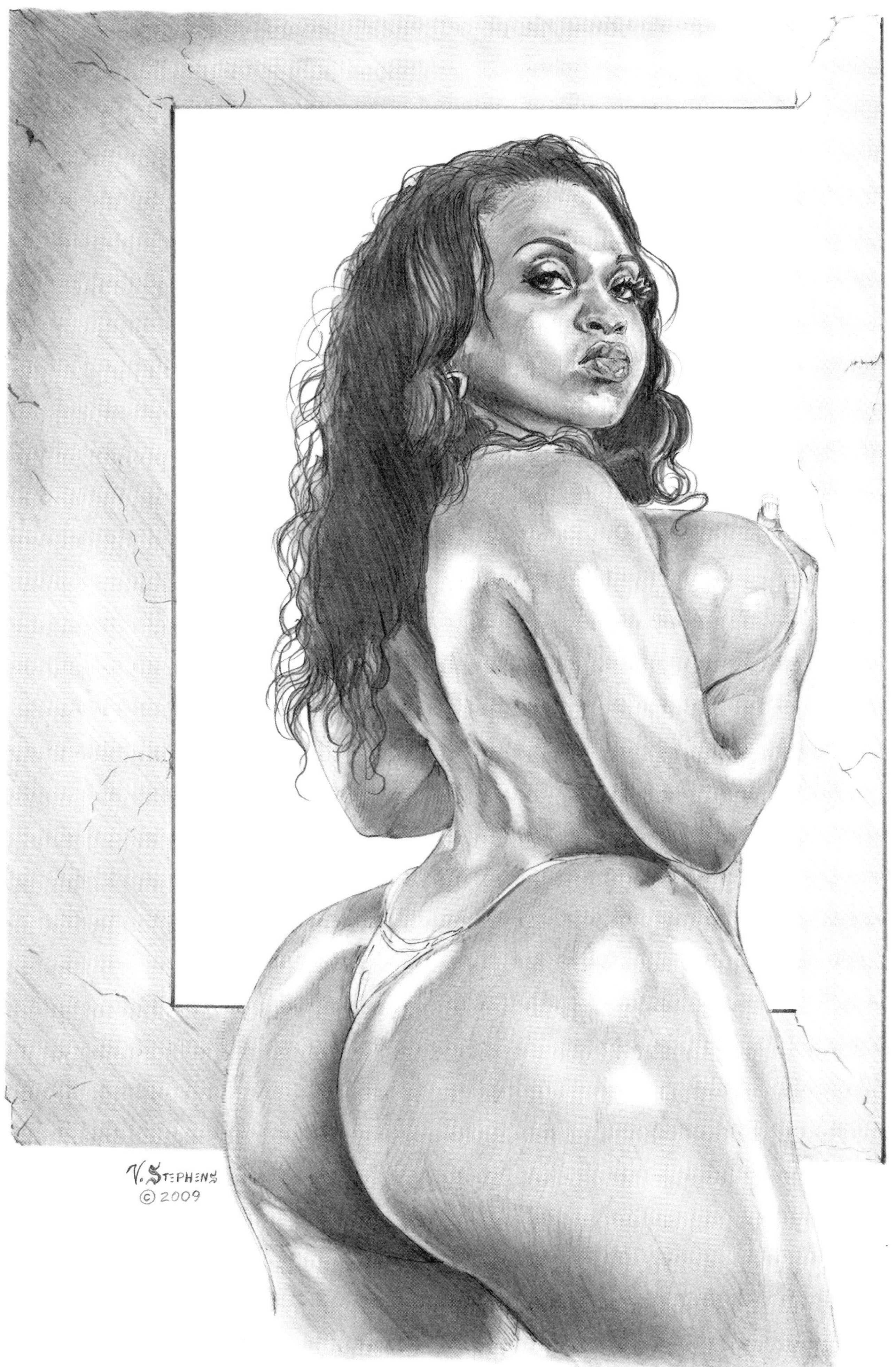
V. STEPHENS
© 2009

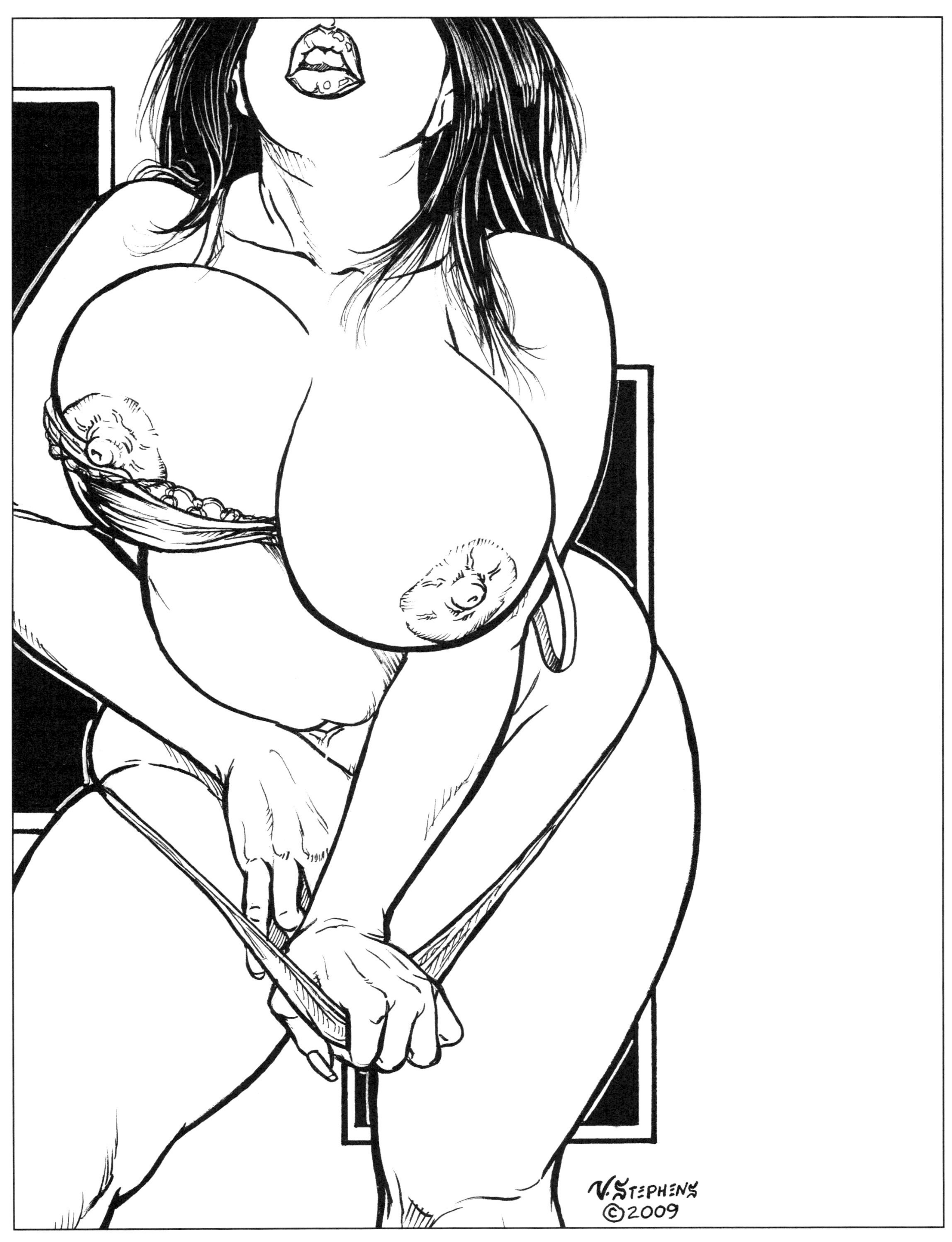
V. STEPHENS
©2009

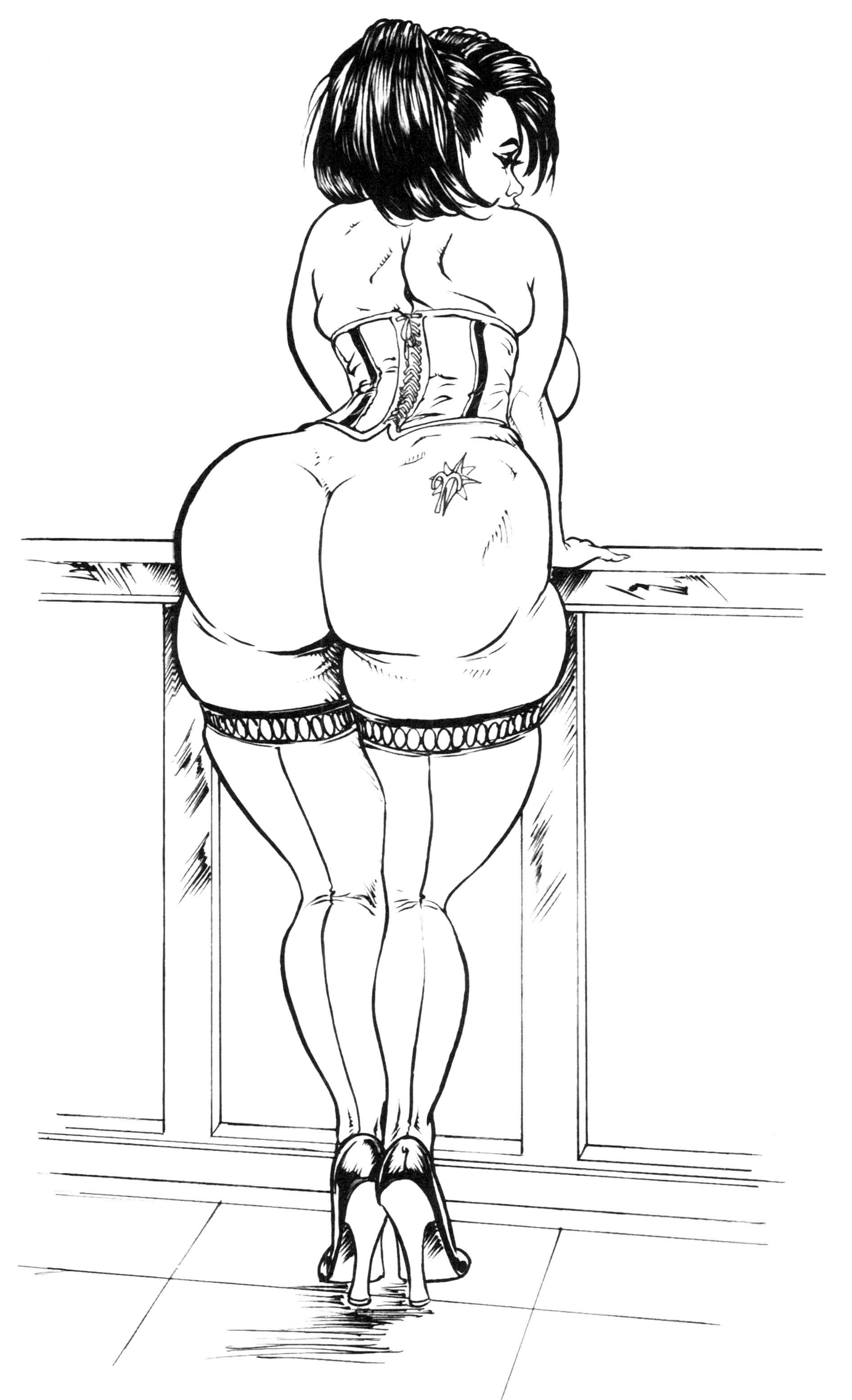

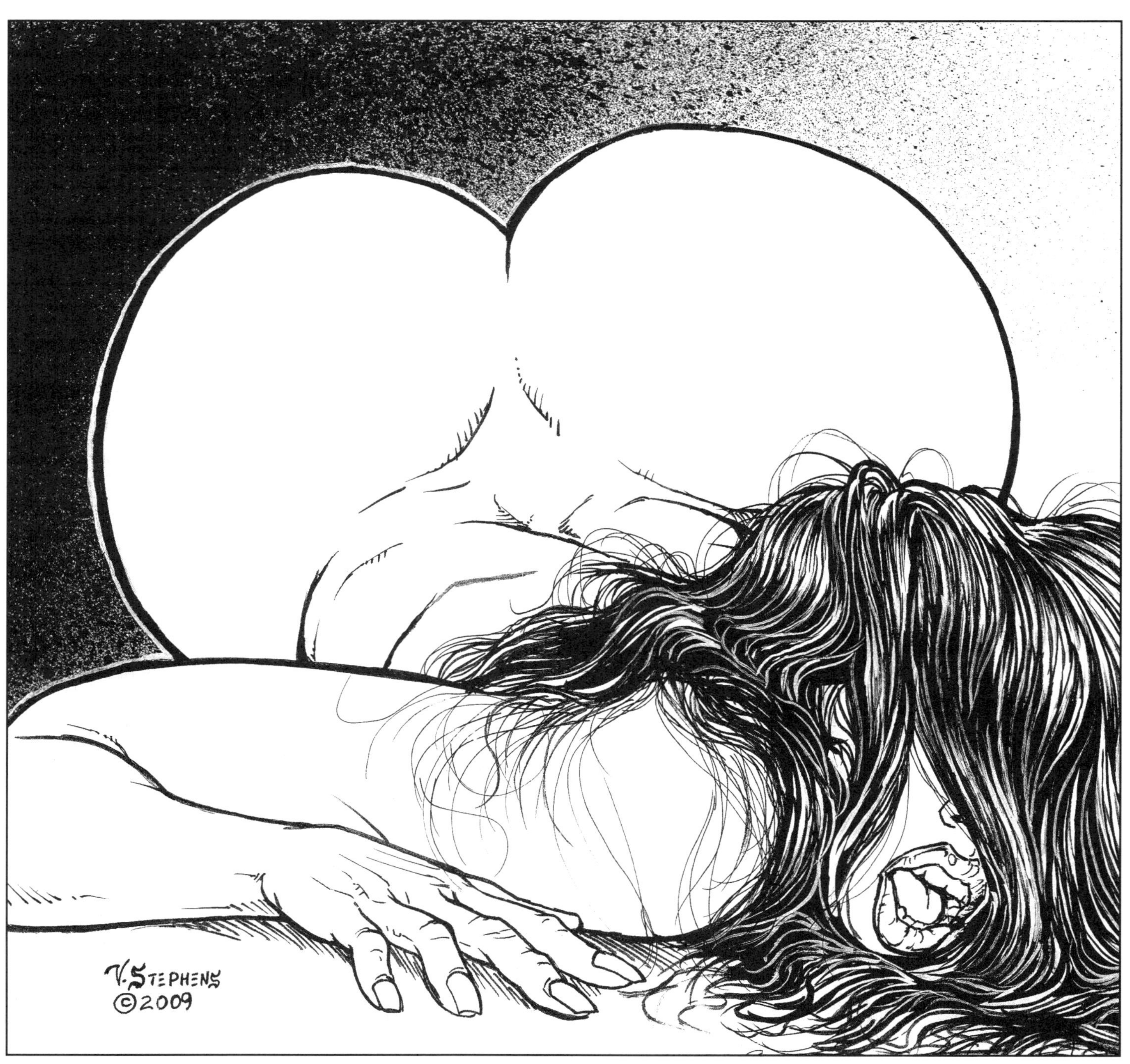
V. STEPHENS
©2009

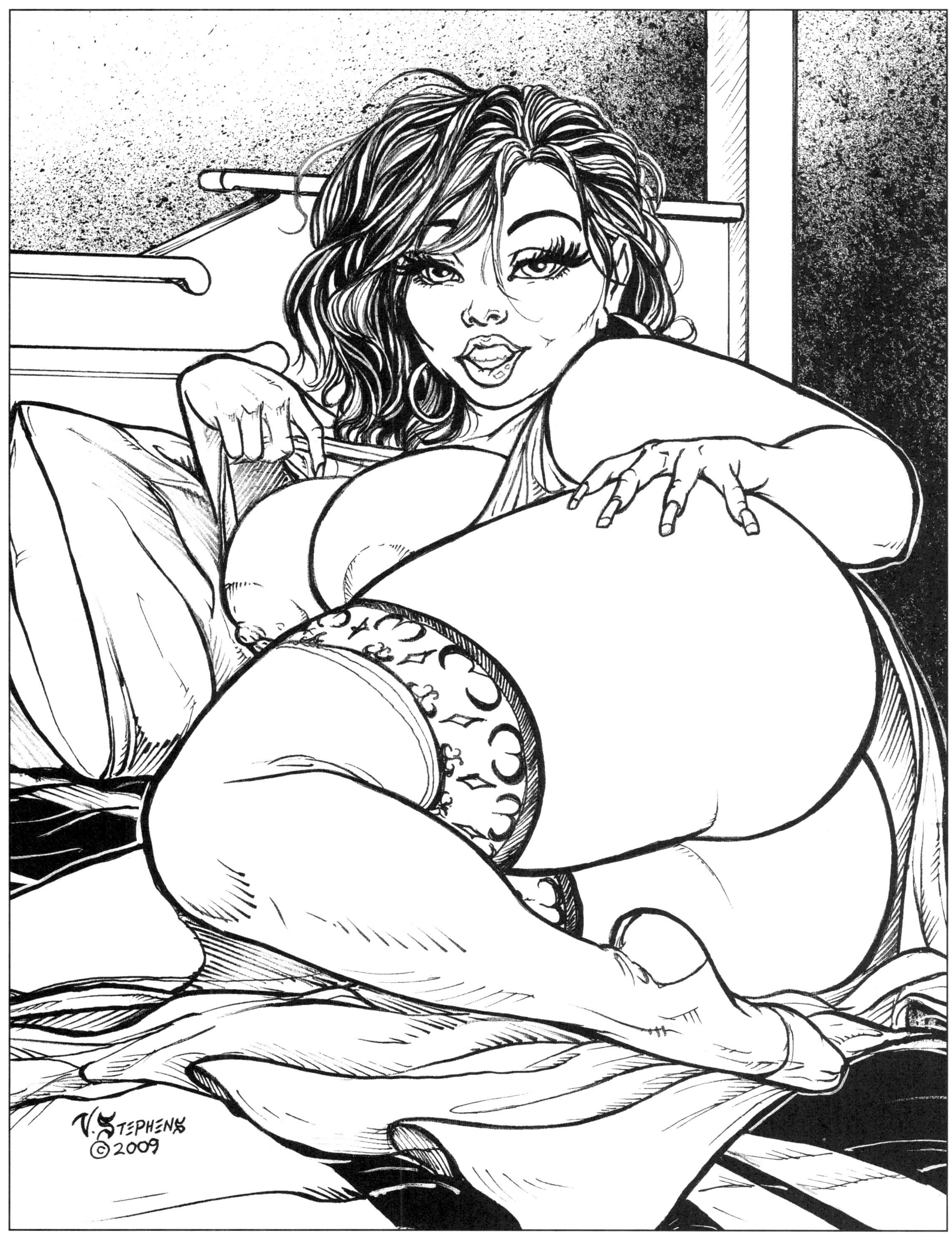
V. STEPHENS
©2009

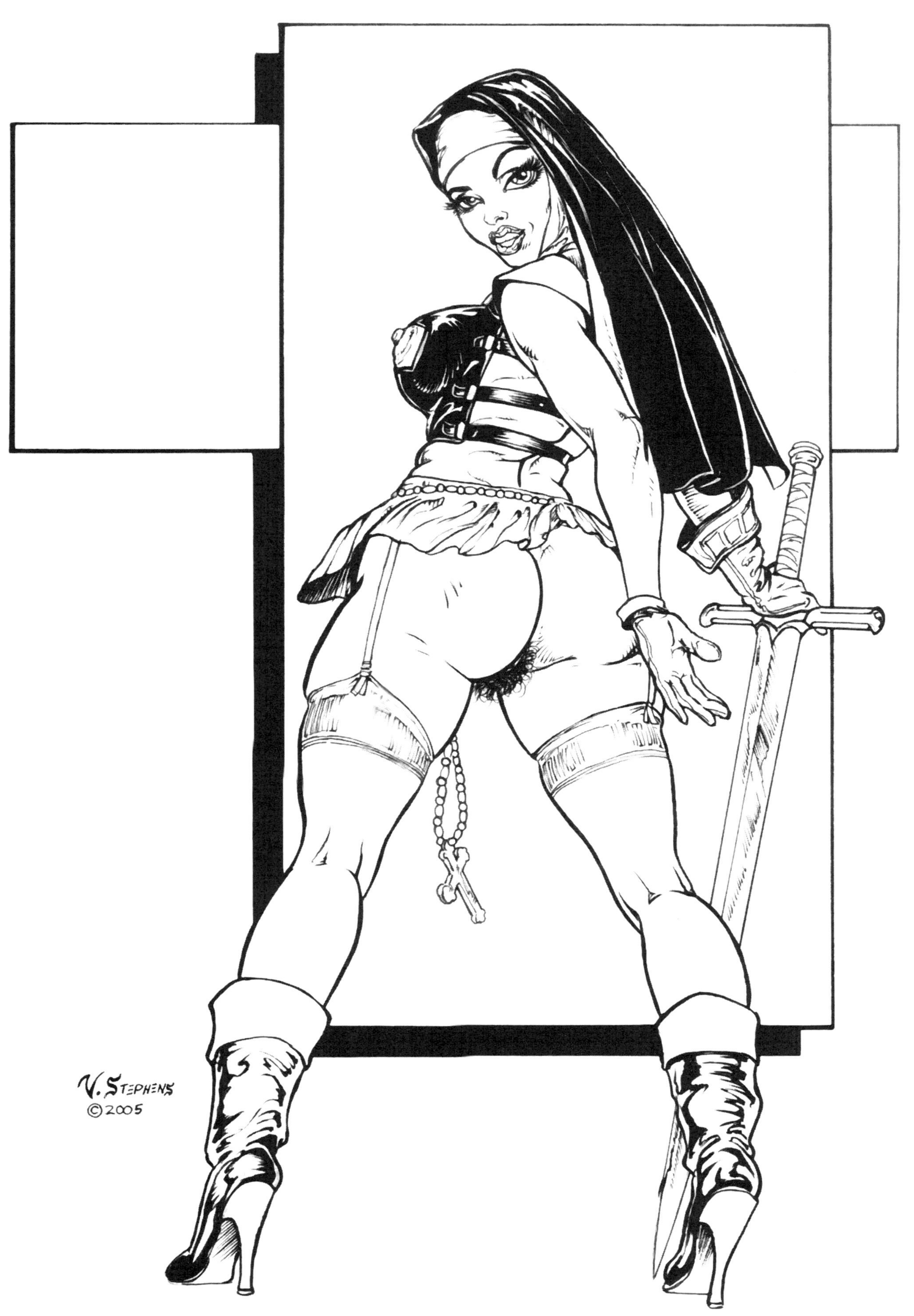
V. Stephens
©2005

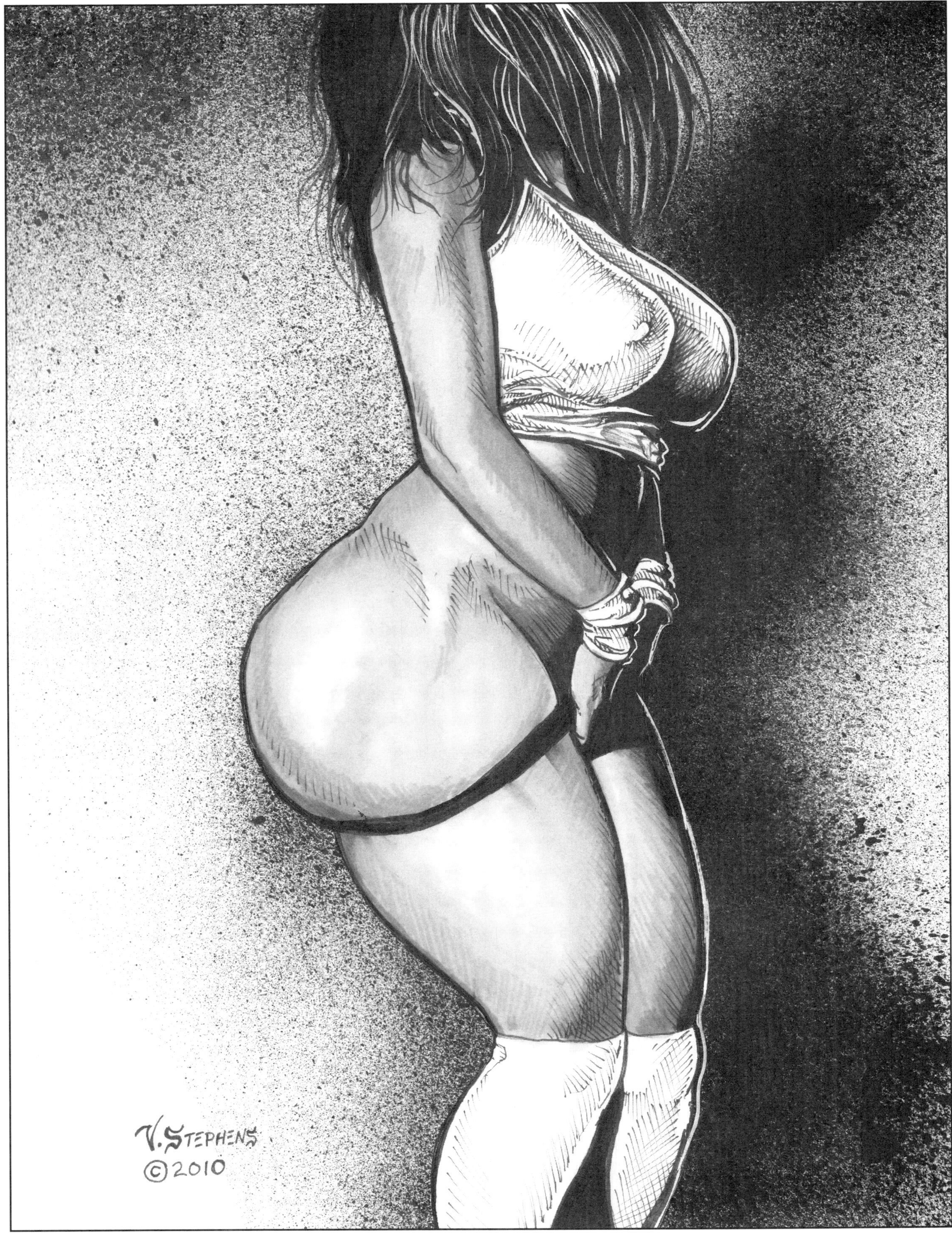
V. STEPHENS
©2010

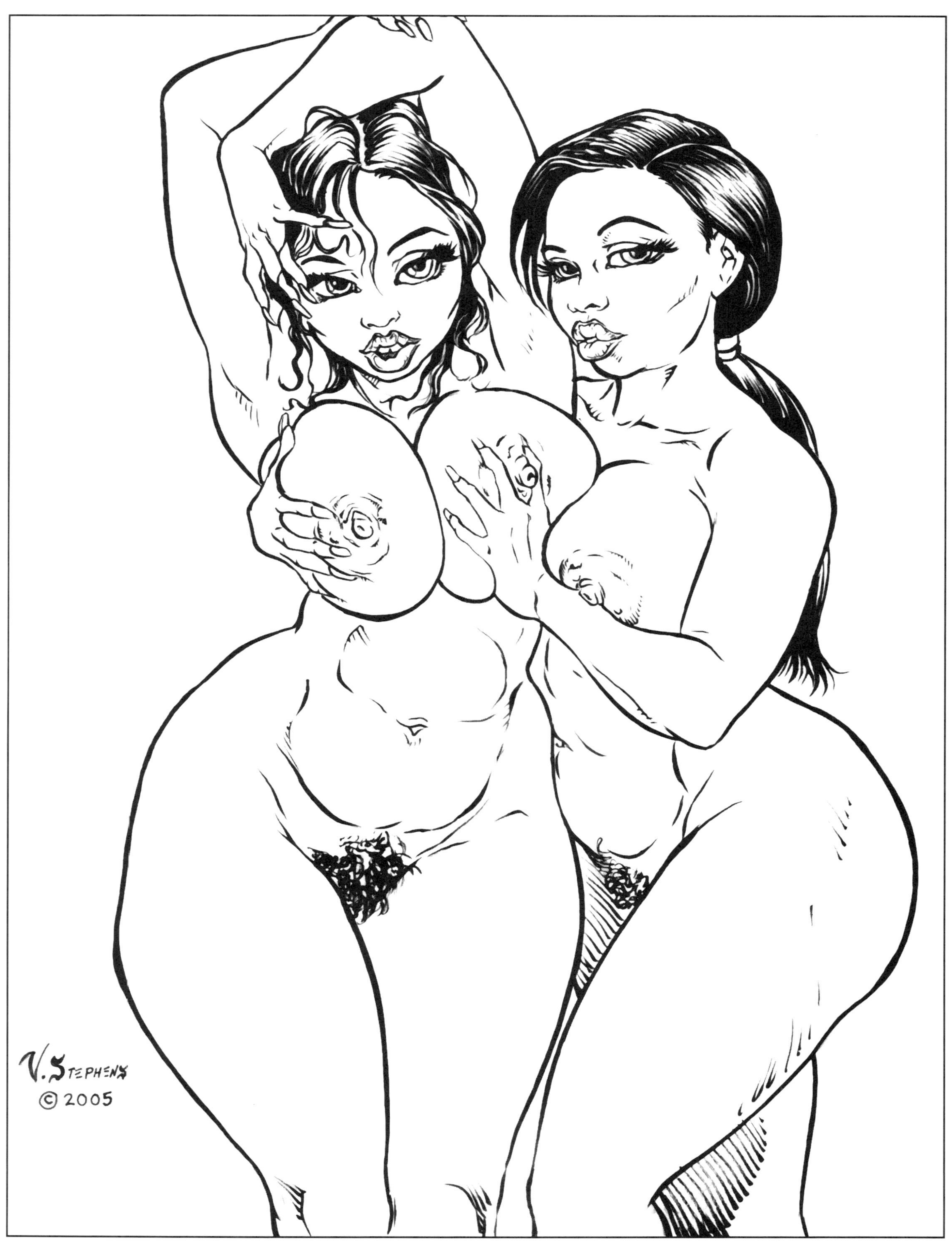
V. Stephens
© 2005

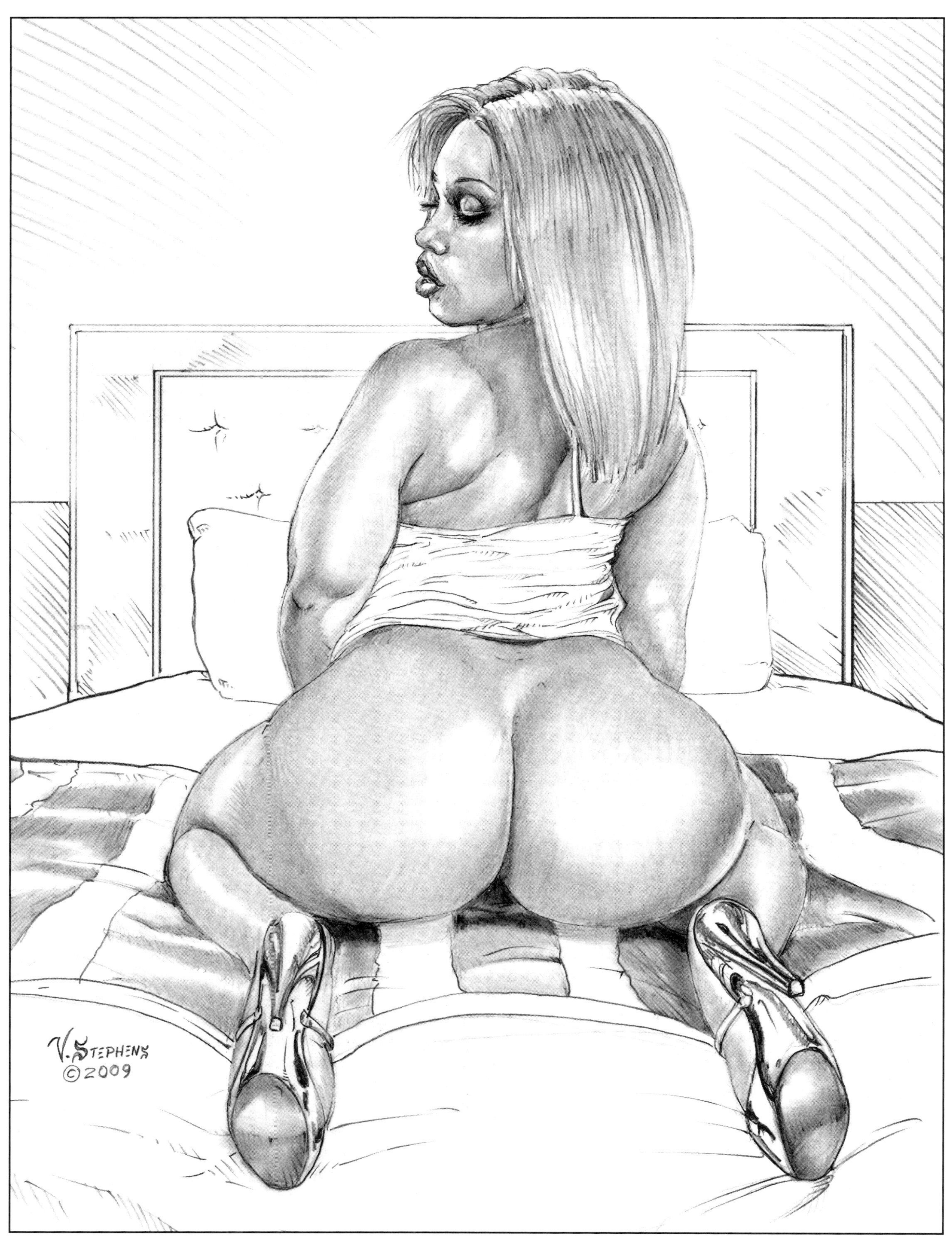
V. Stephens
©2009

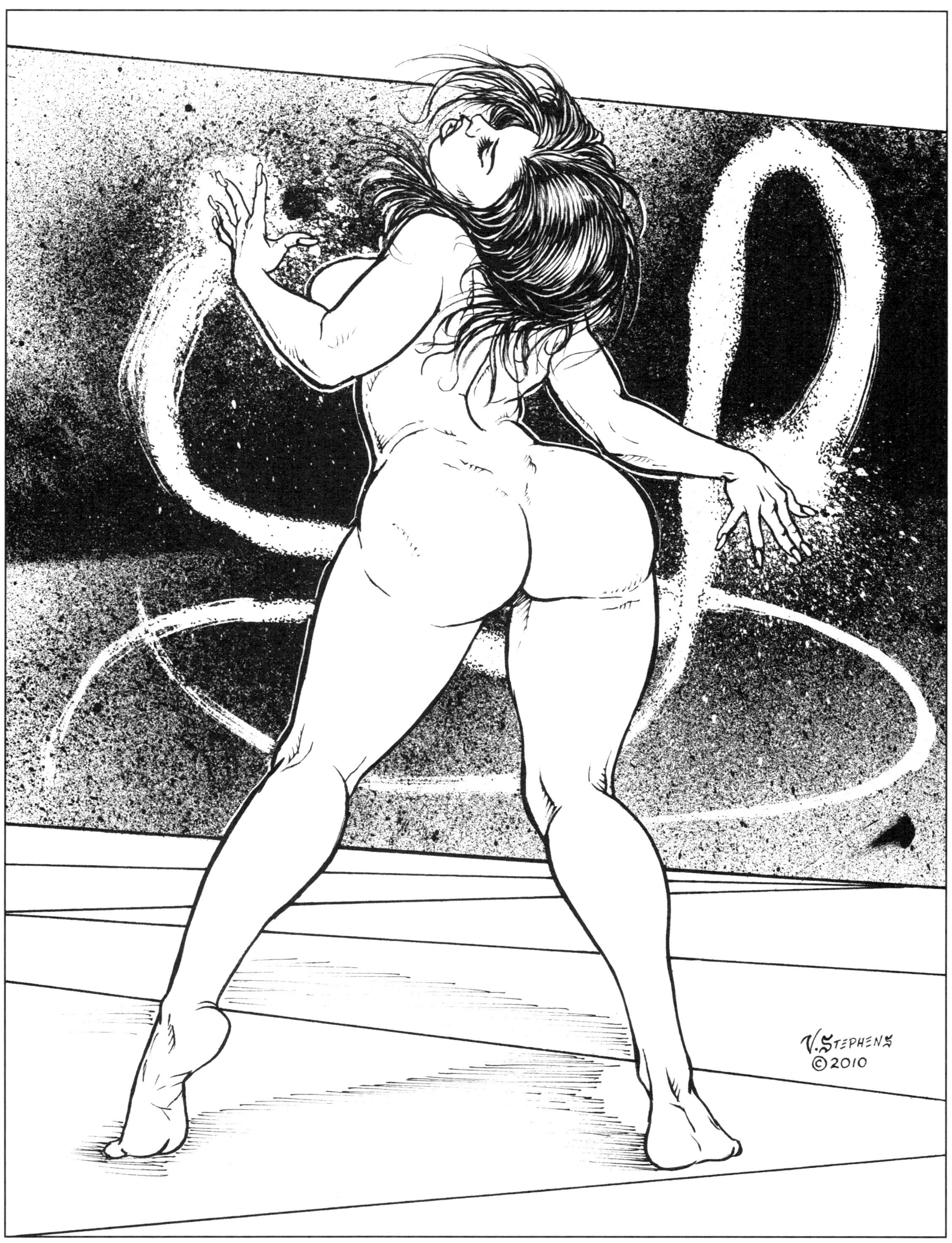
V. STEPHENS
©2010

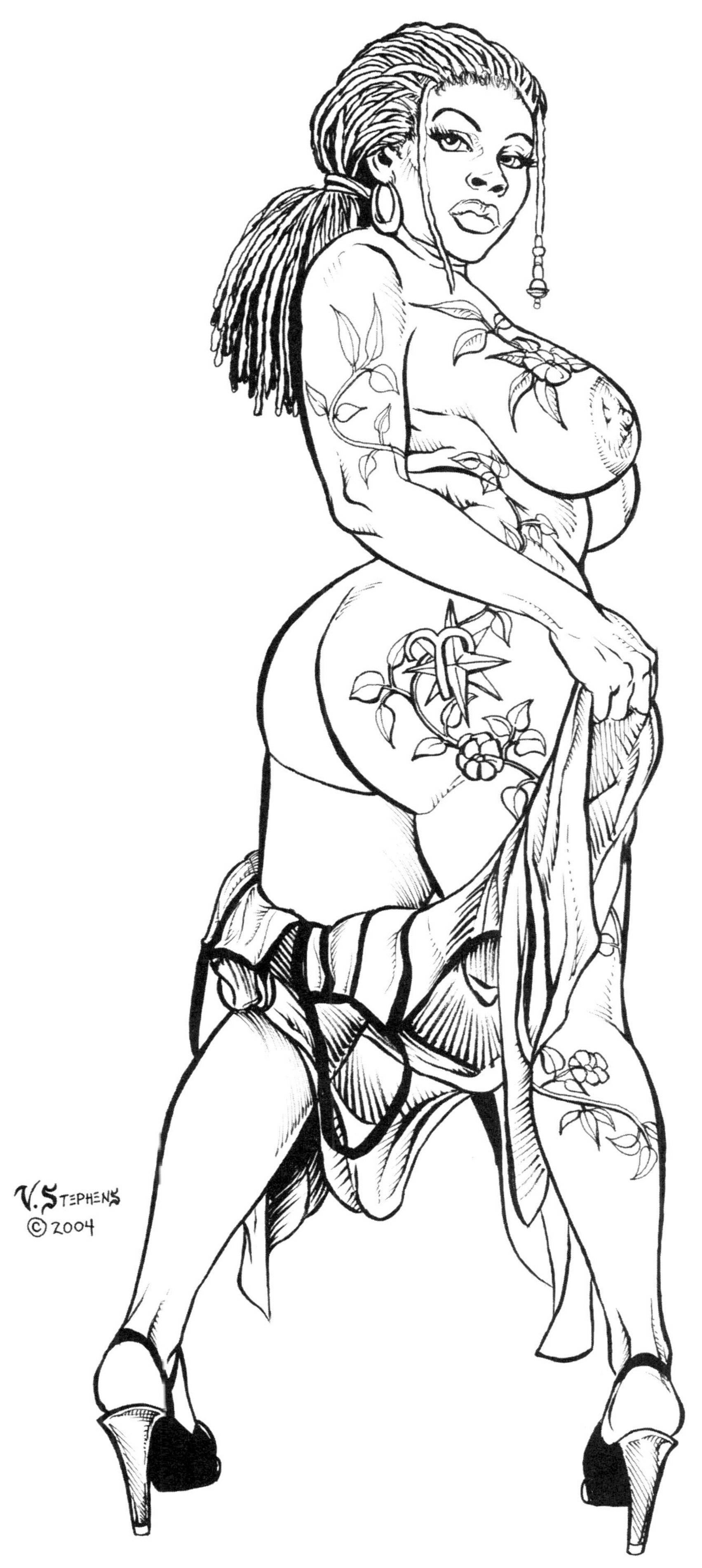
V. Stephens
©2004

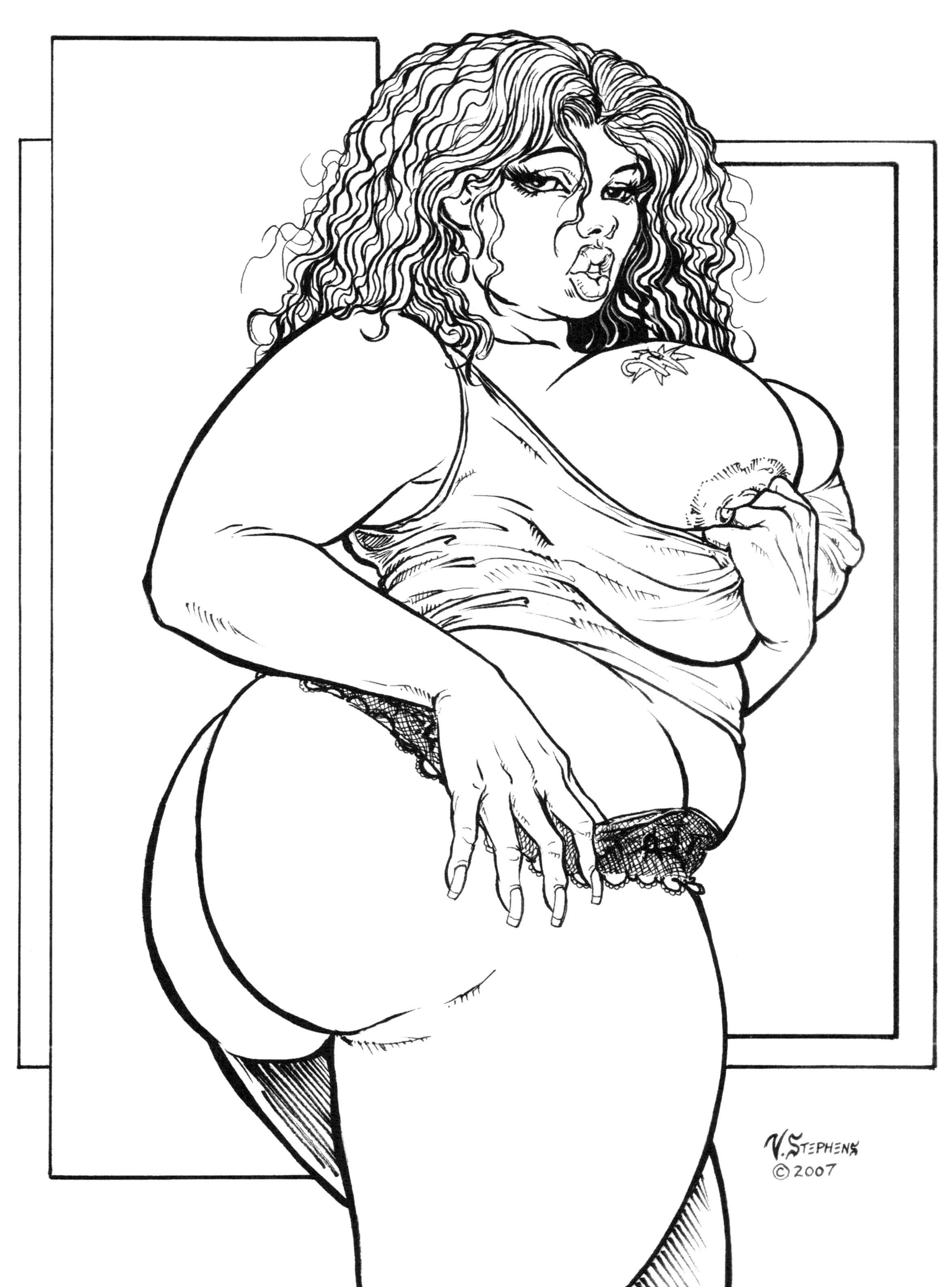
V. STEPHENS
©2007

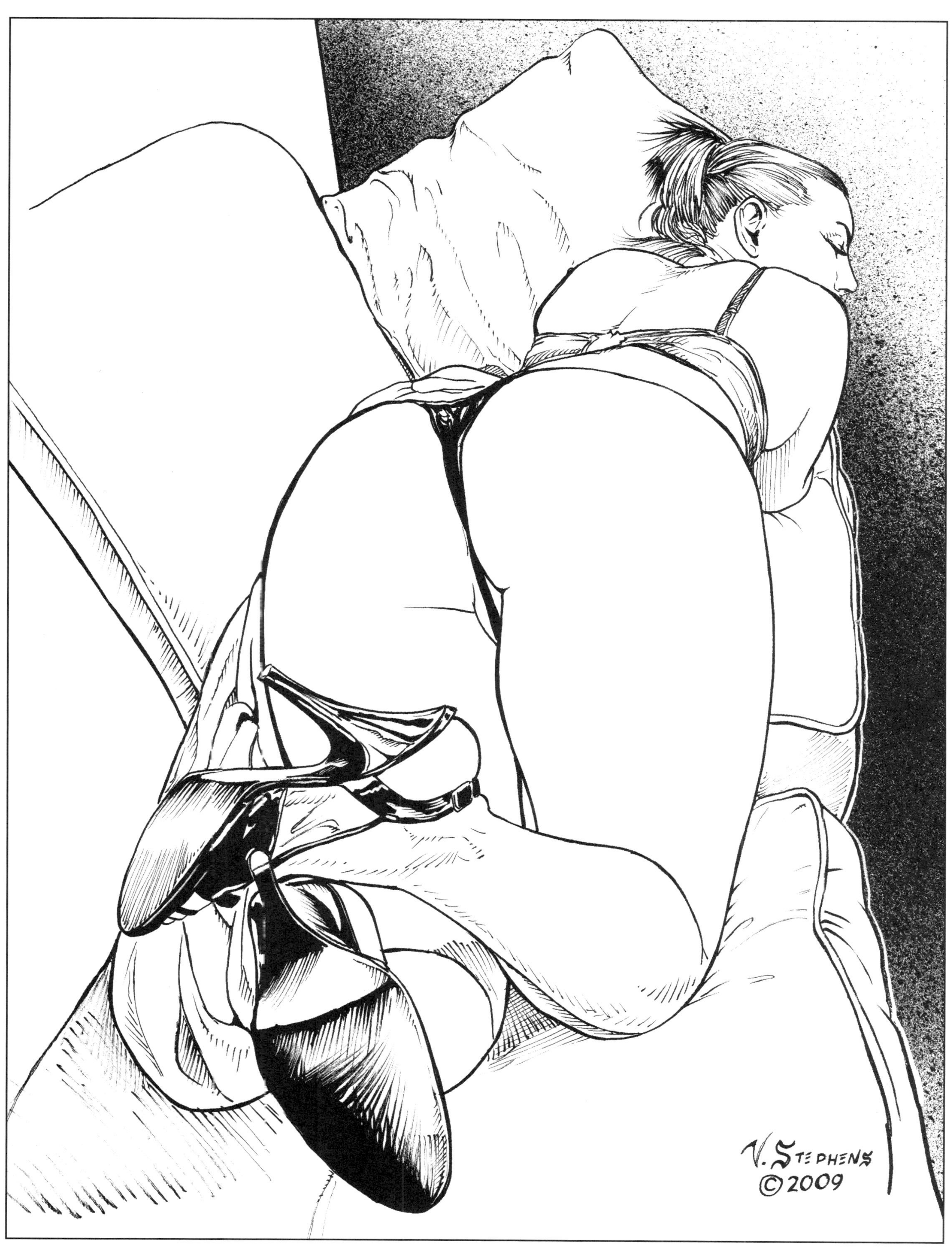
V. STEPHENS
©2009

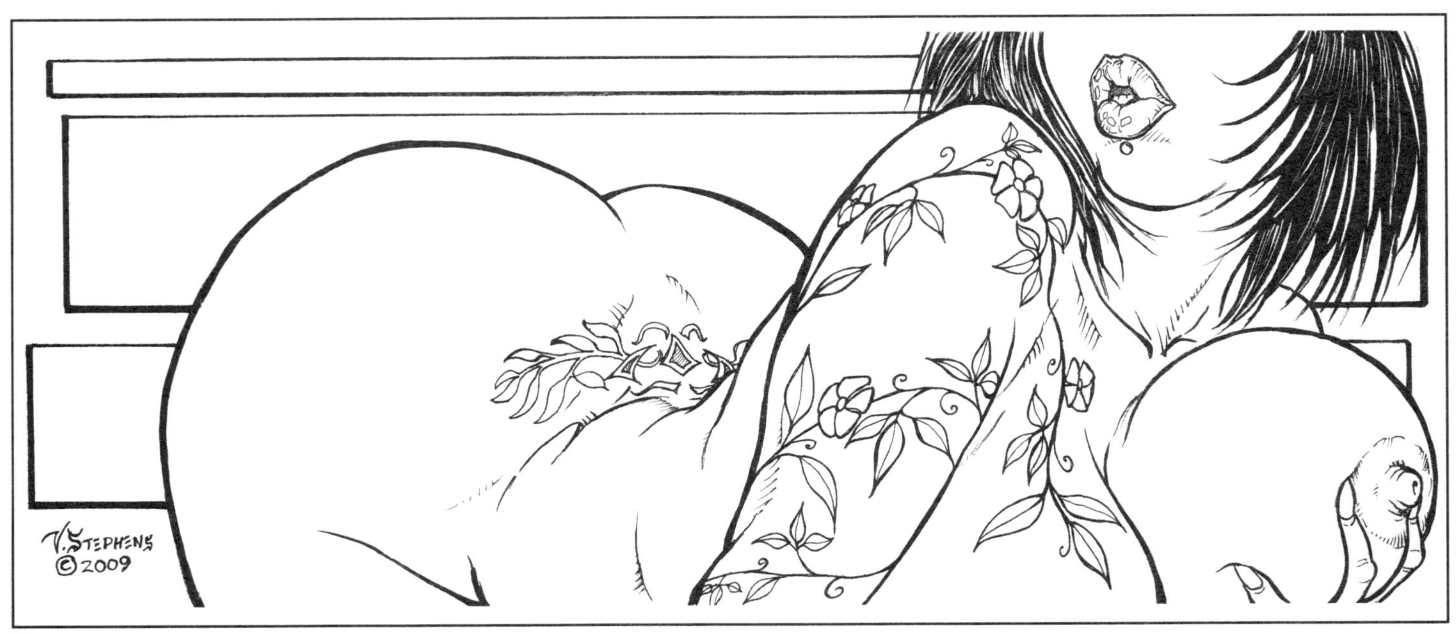

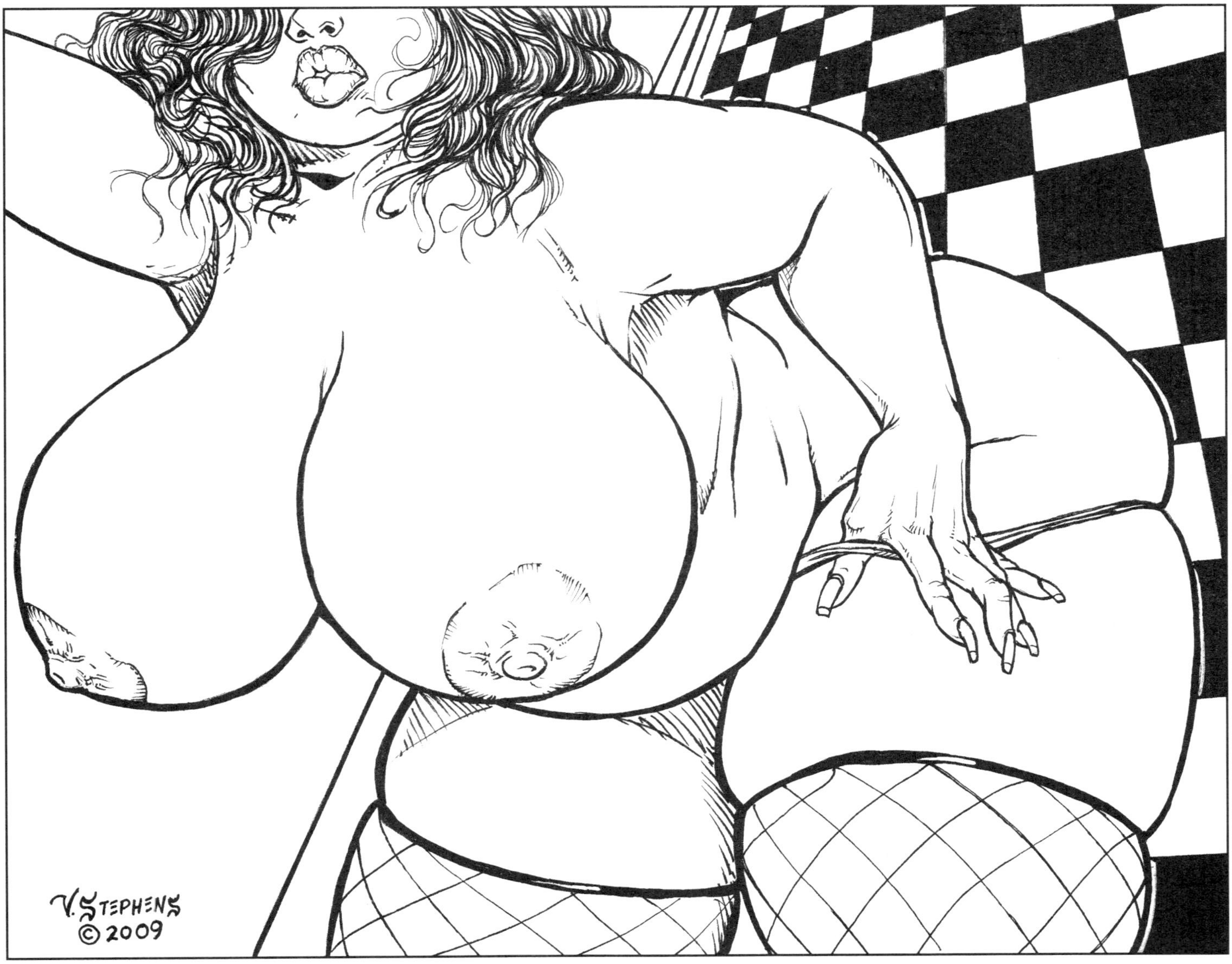

V. STEPHENS
©2009

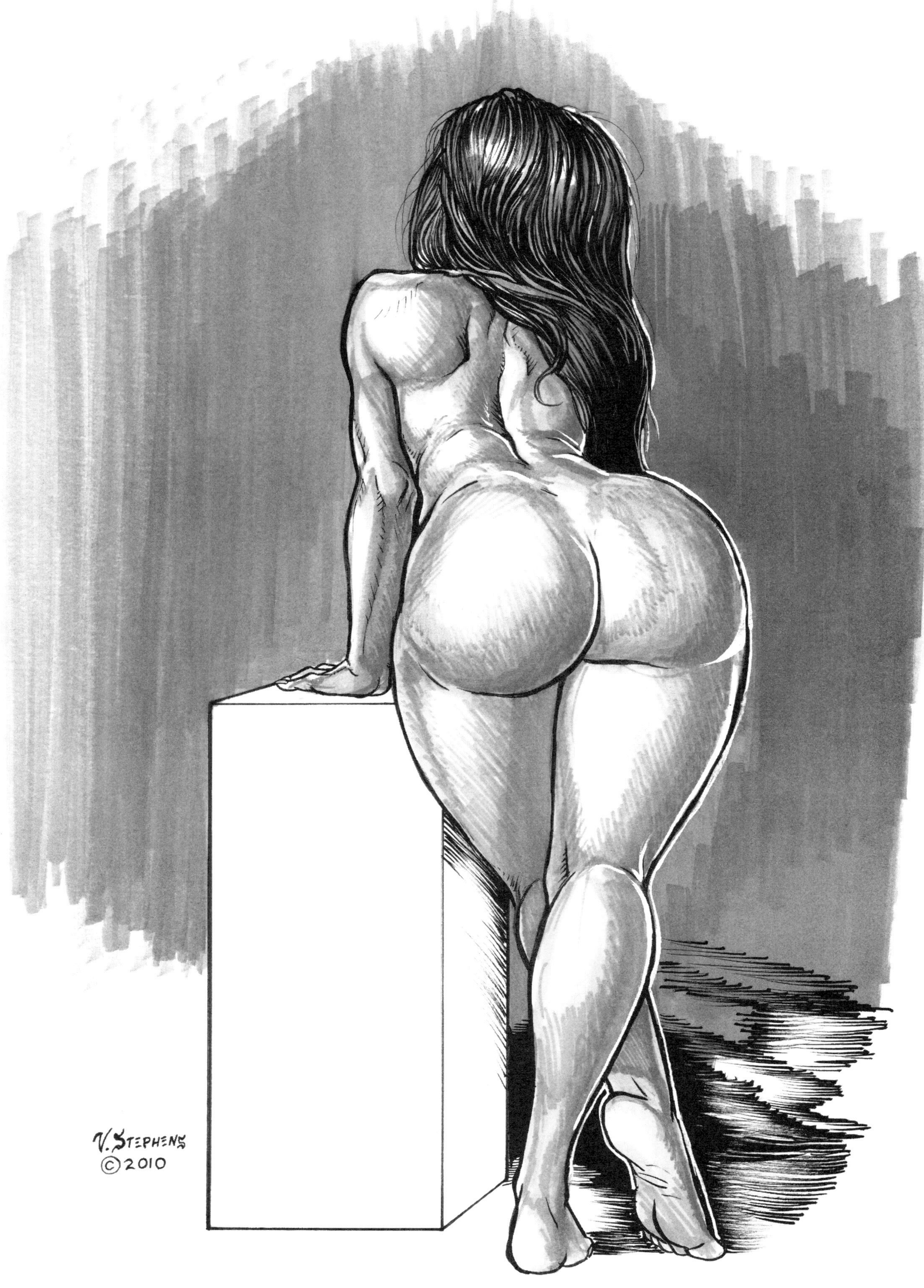
V. STEPHENS
©2010

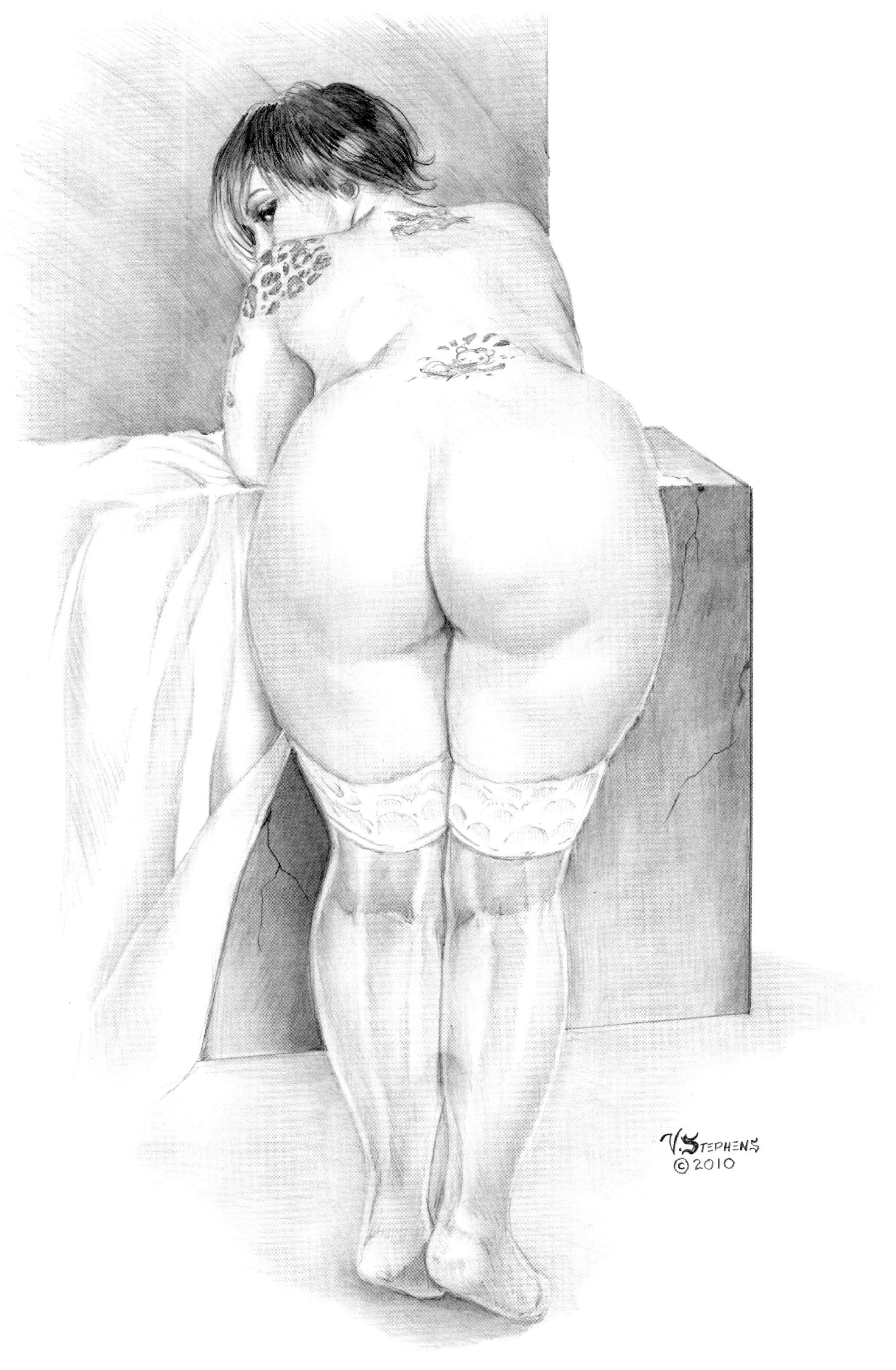
V. Stephens
©2010

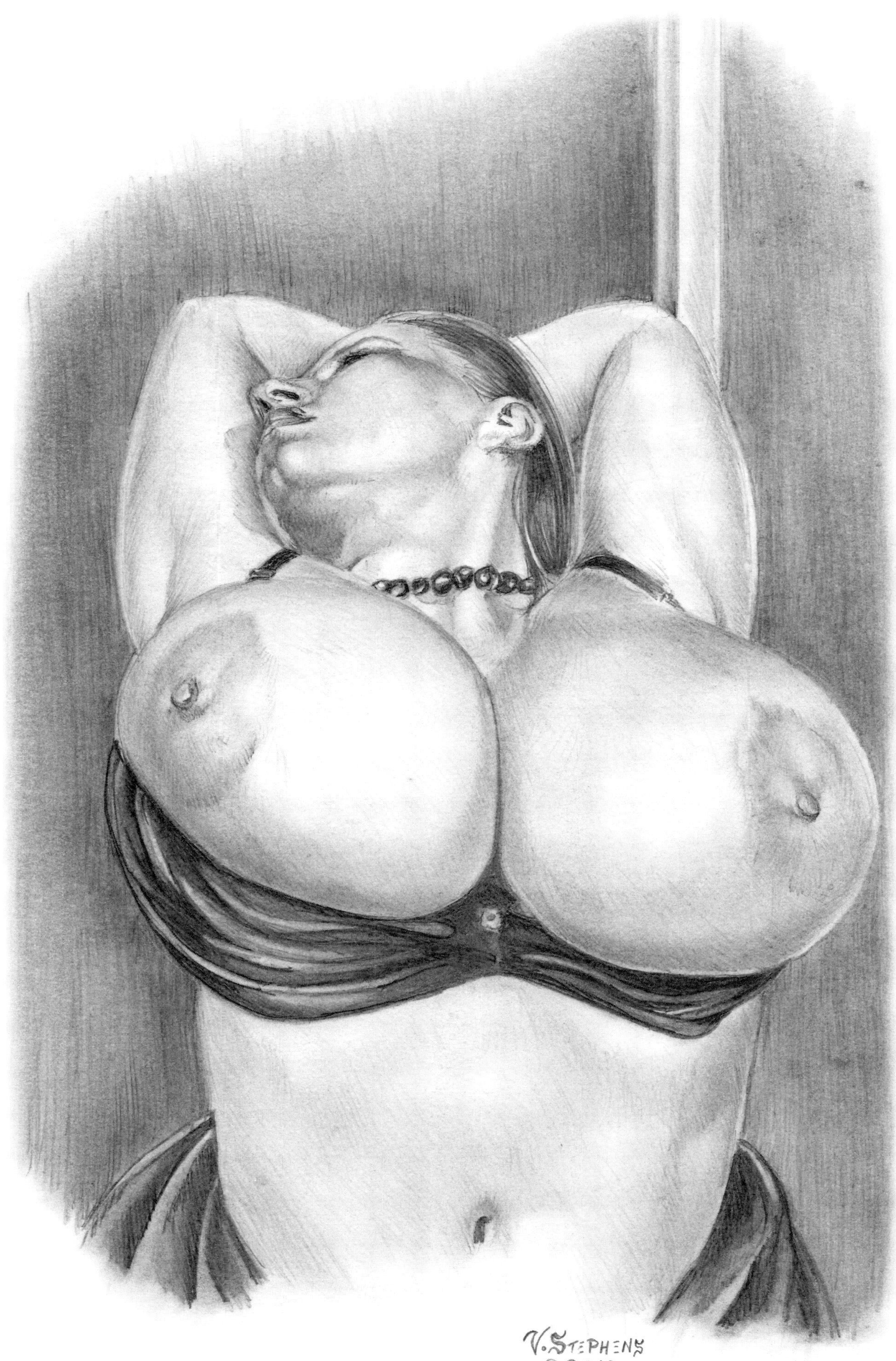
V. STEPHENS
©2010

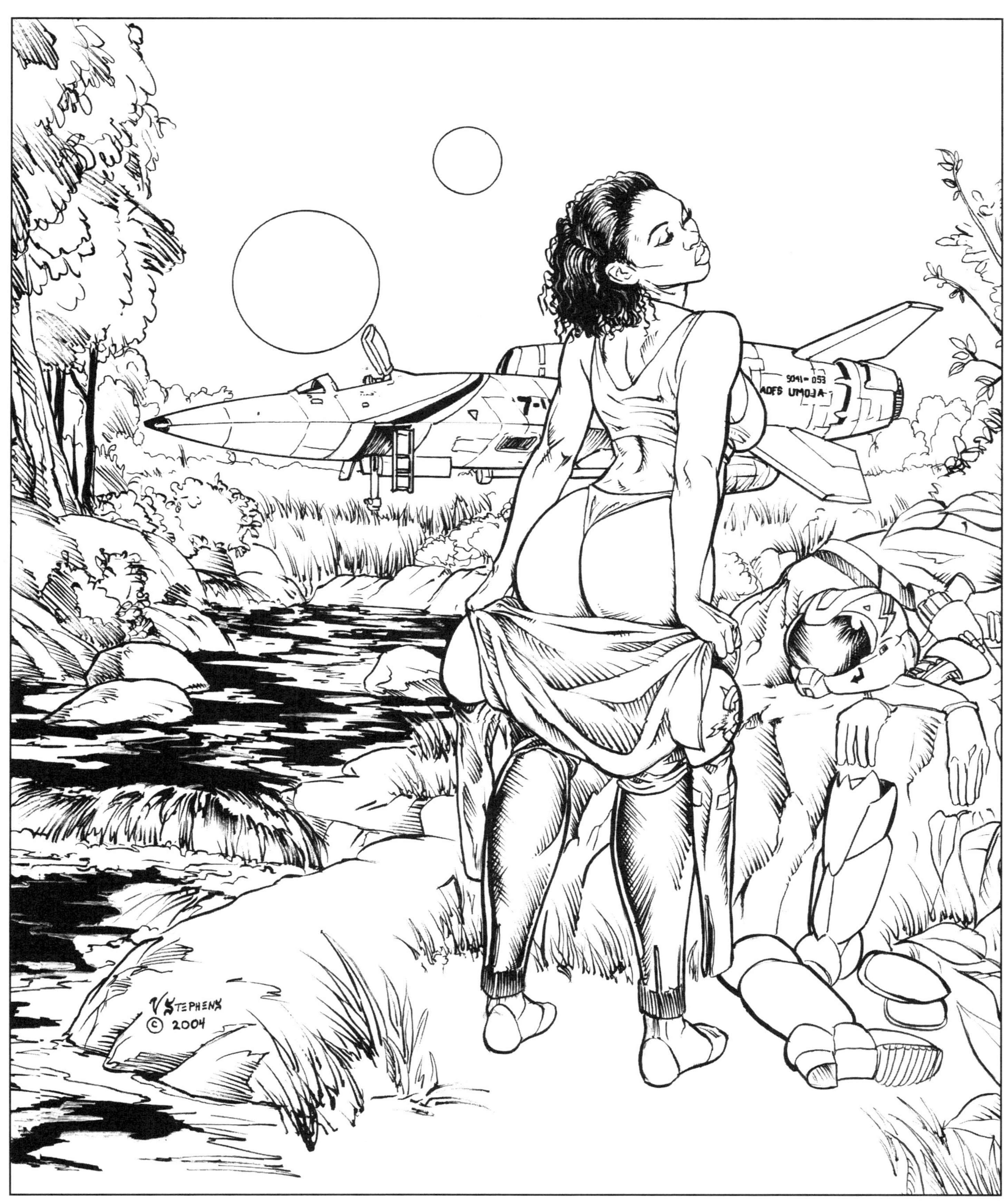
5041-053
ADFS UMOJA
V STEPHENS
© 2004

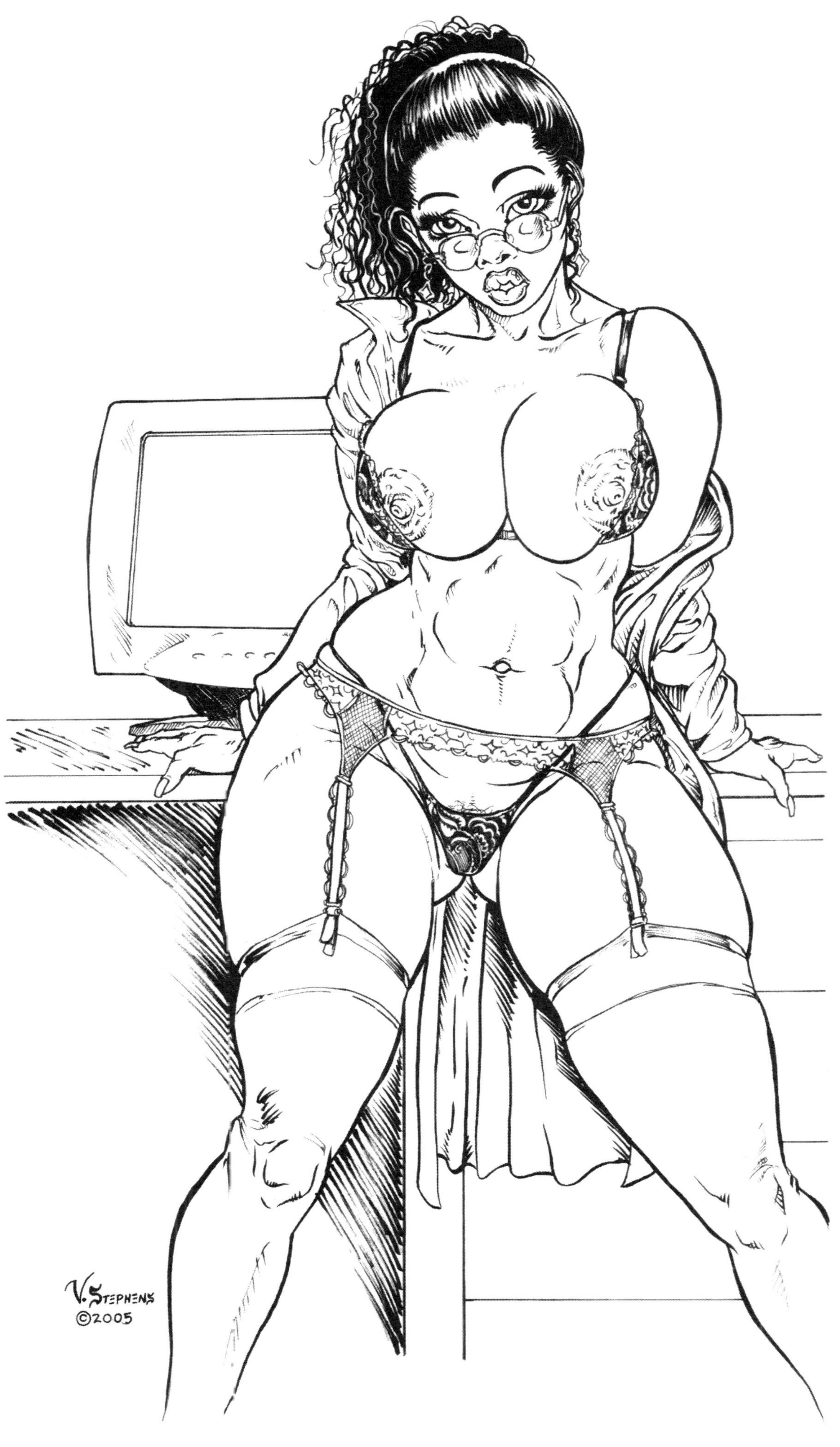
V. STEPHENS
©2005

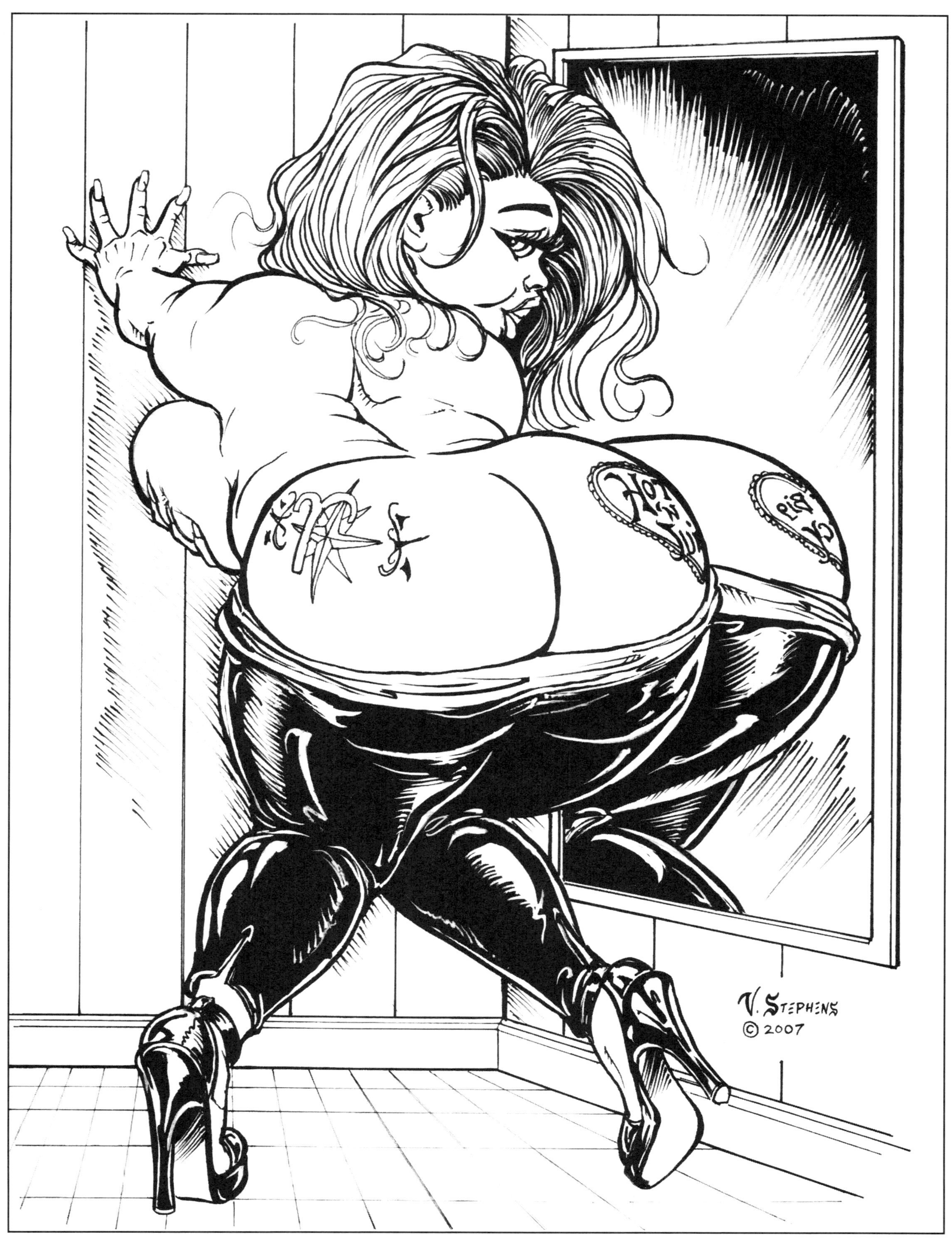
V. Stephens
© 2007

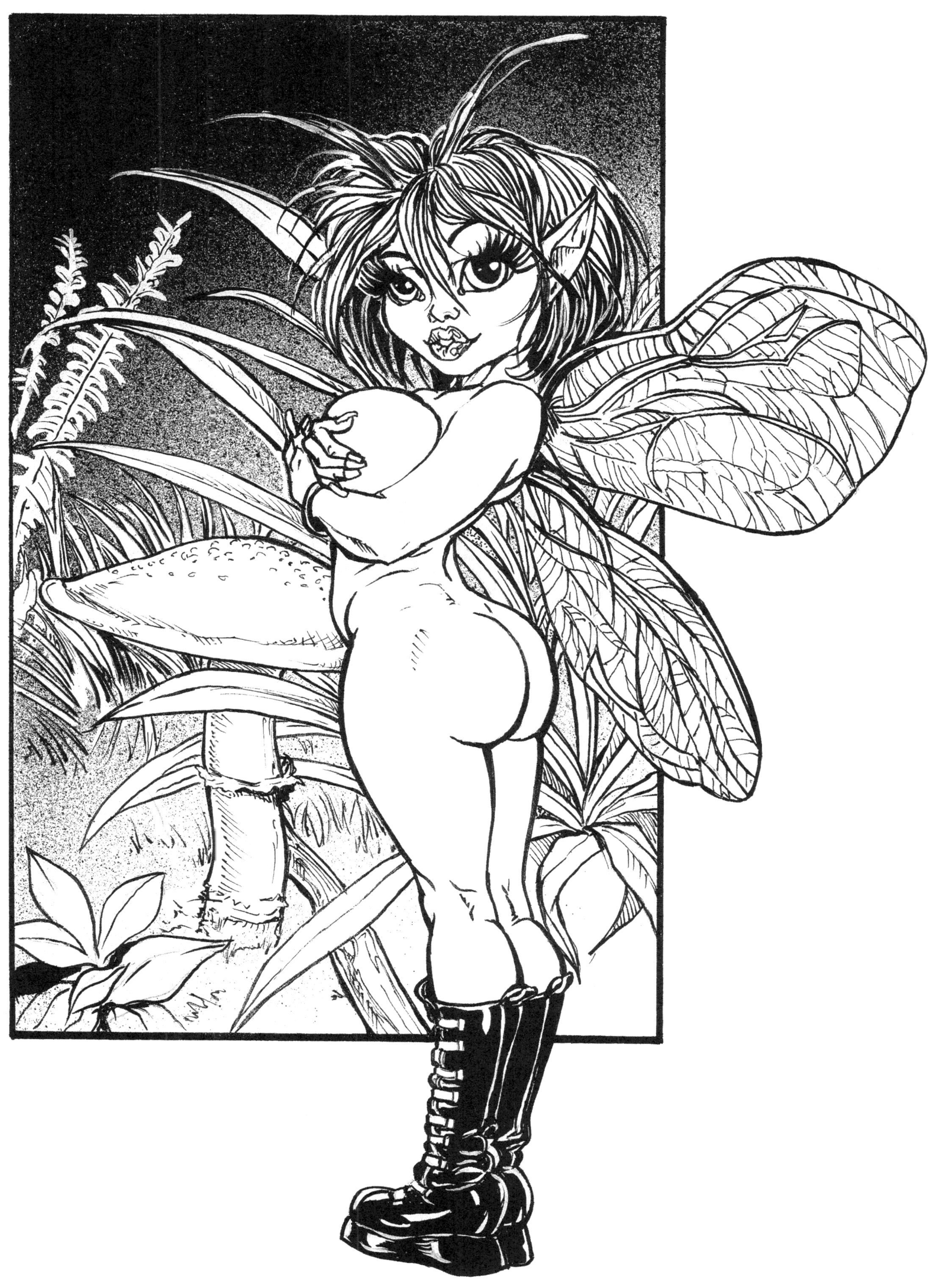

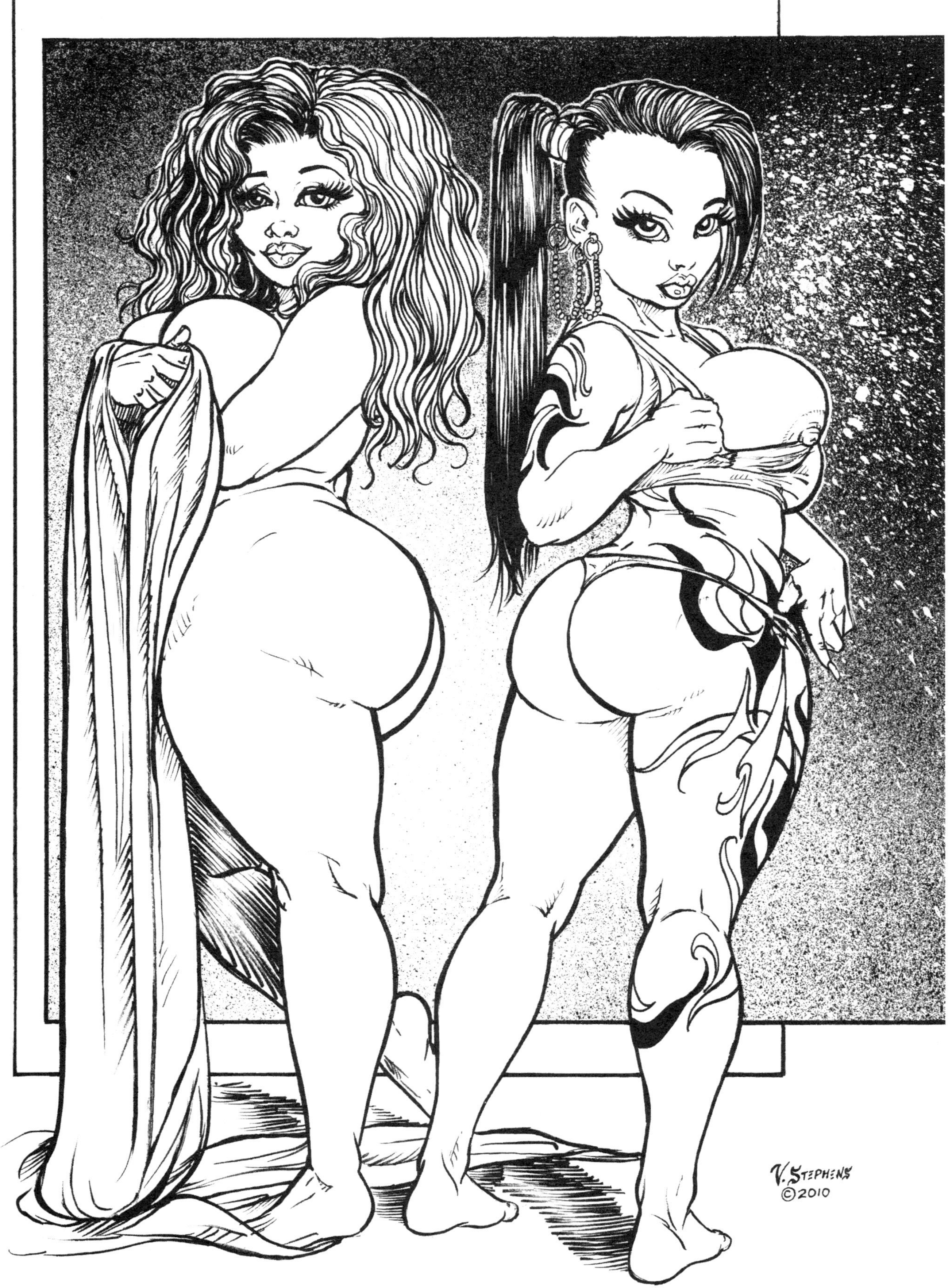
V. Stephens
©2010

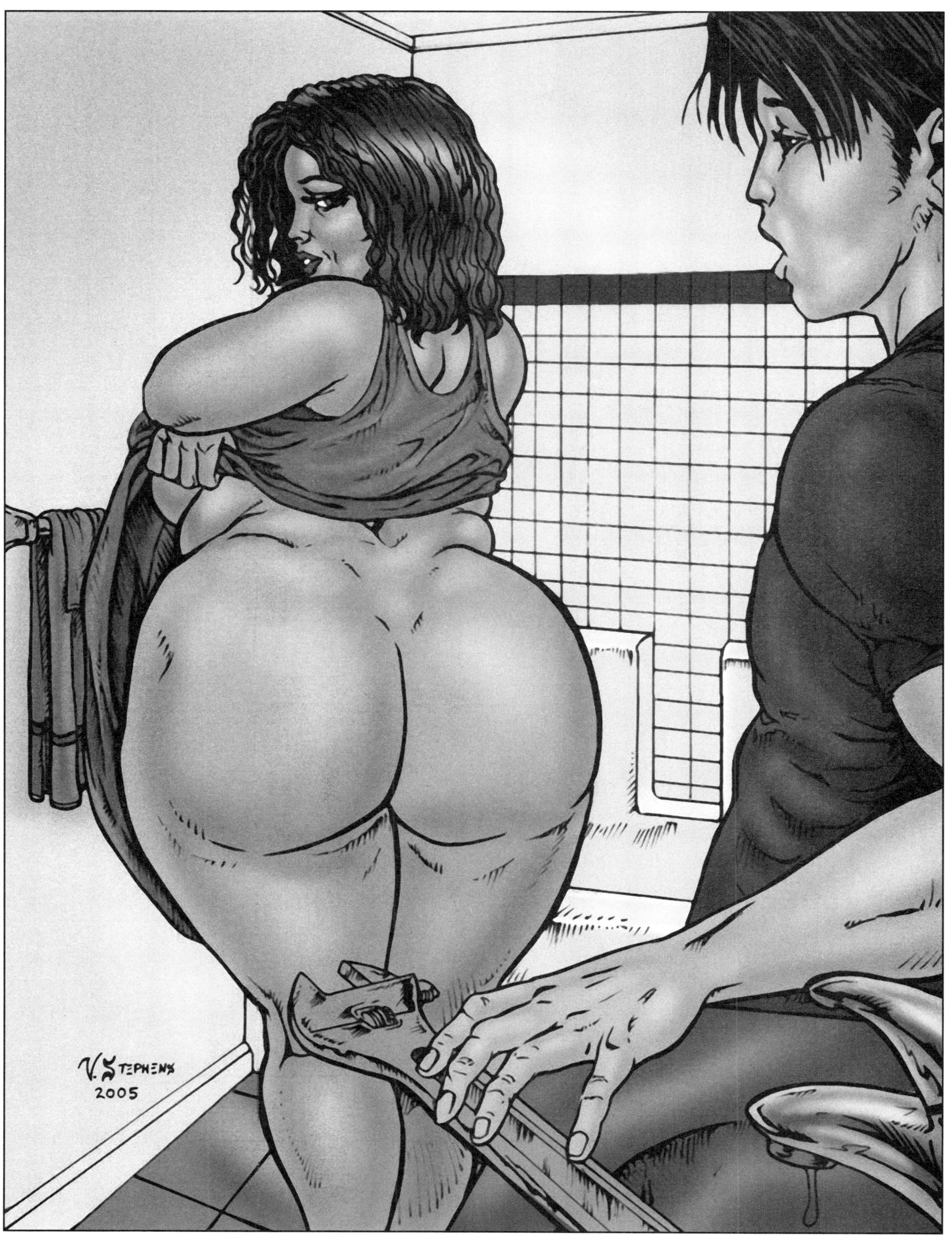
V. STEPHENS
2005

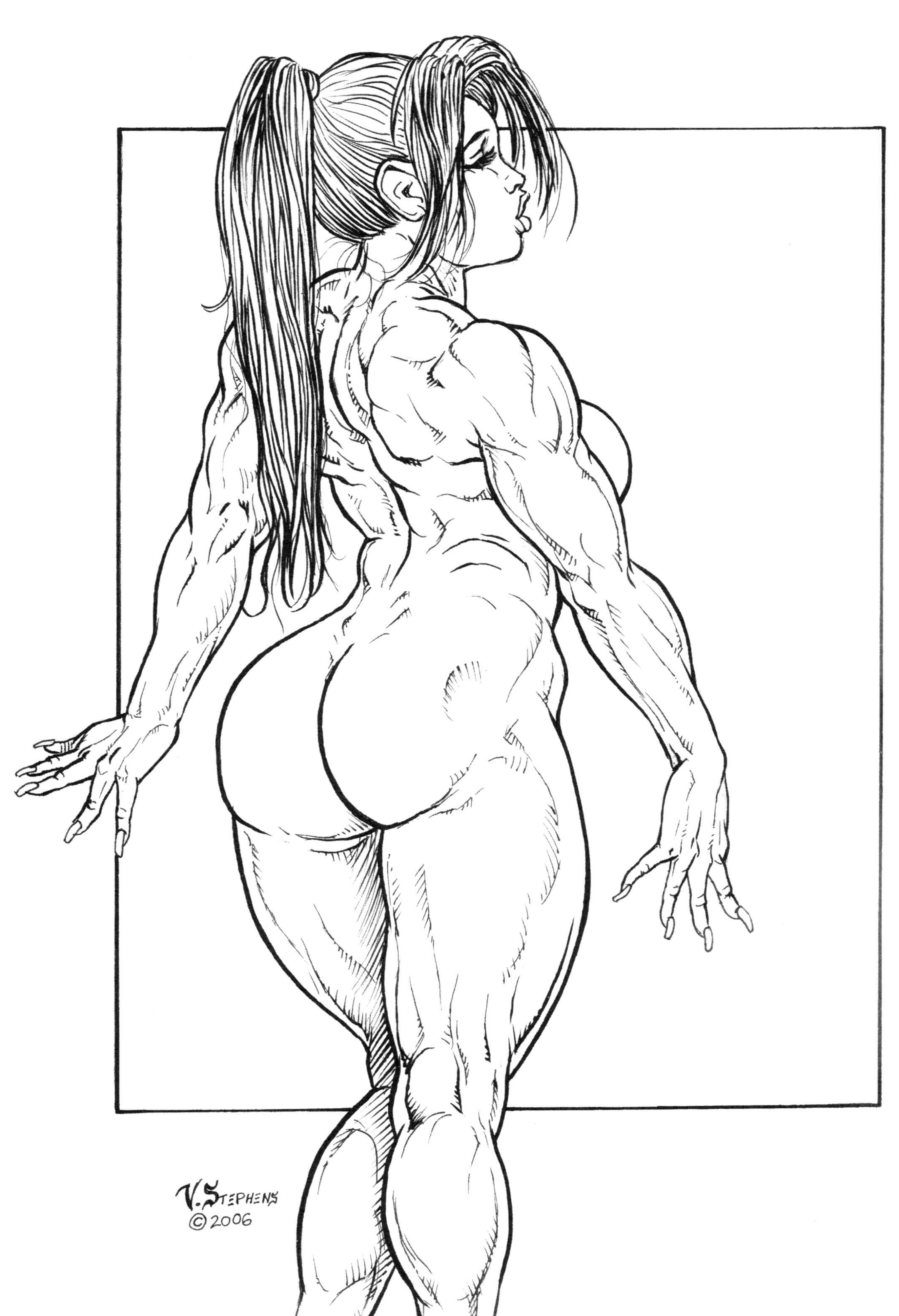
V. Stephens
©2006

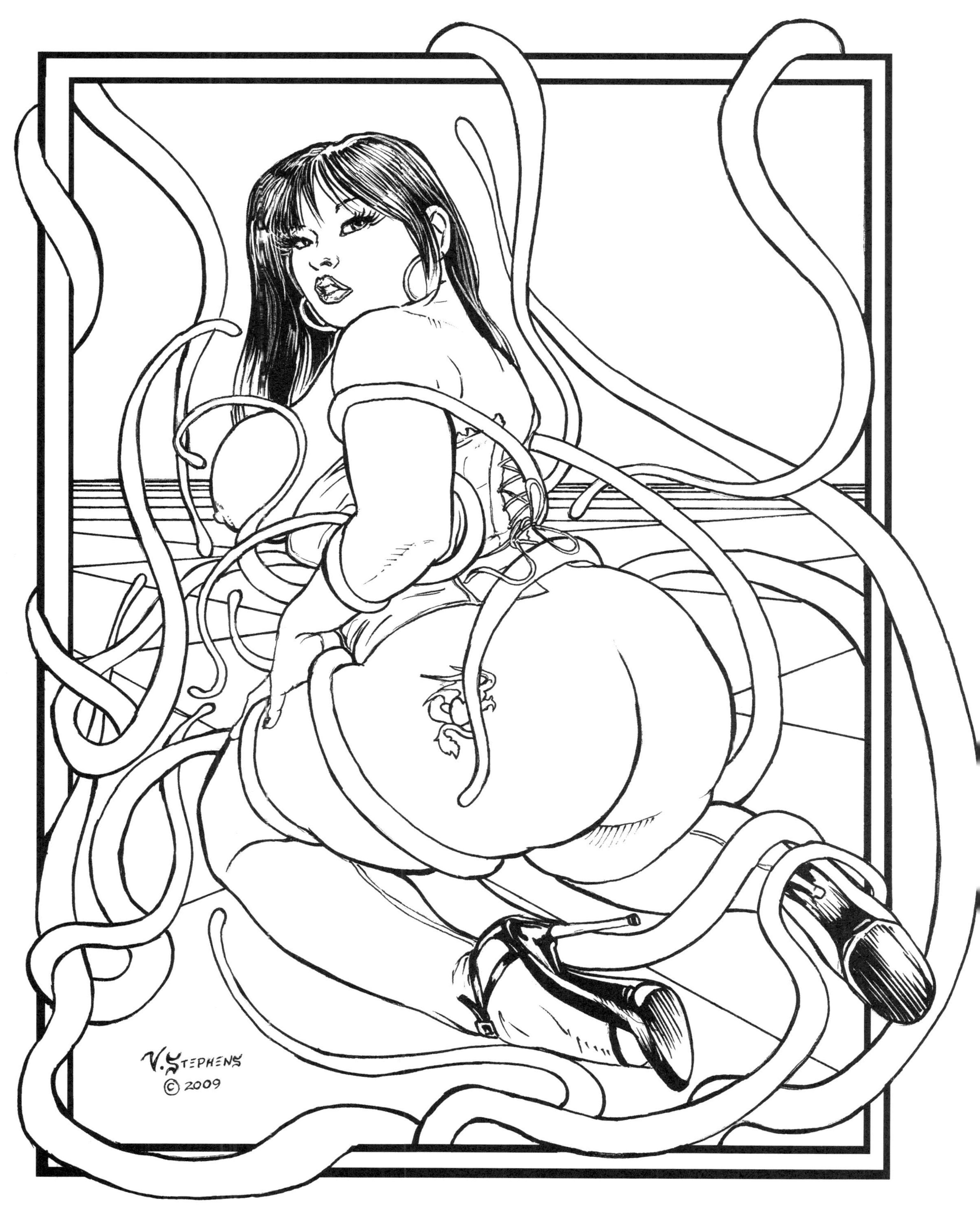
V. Stephens
© 2009

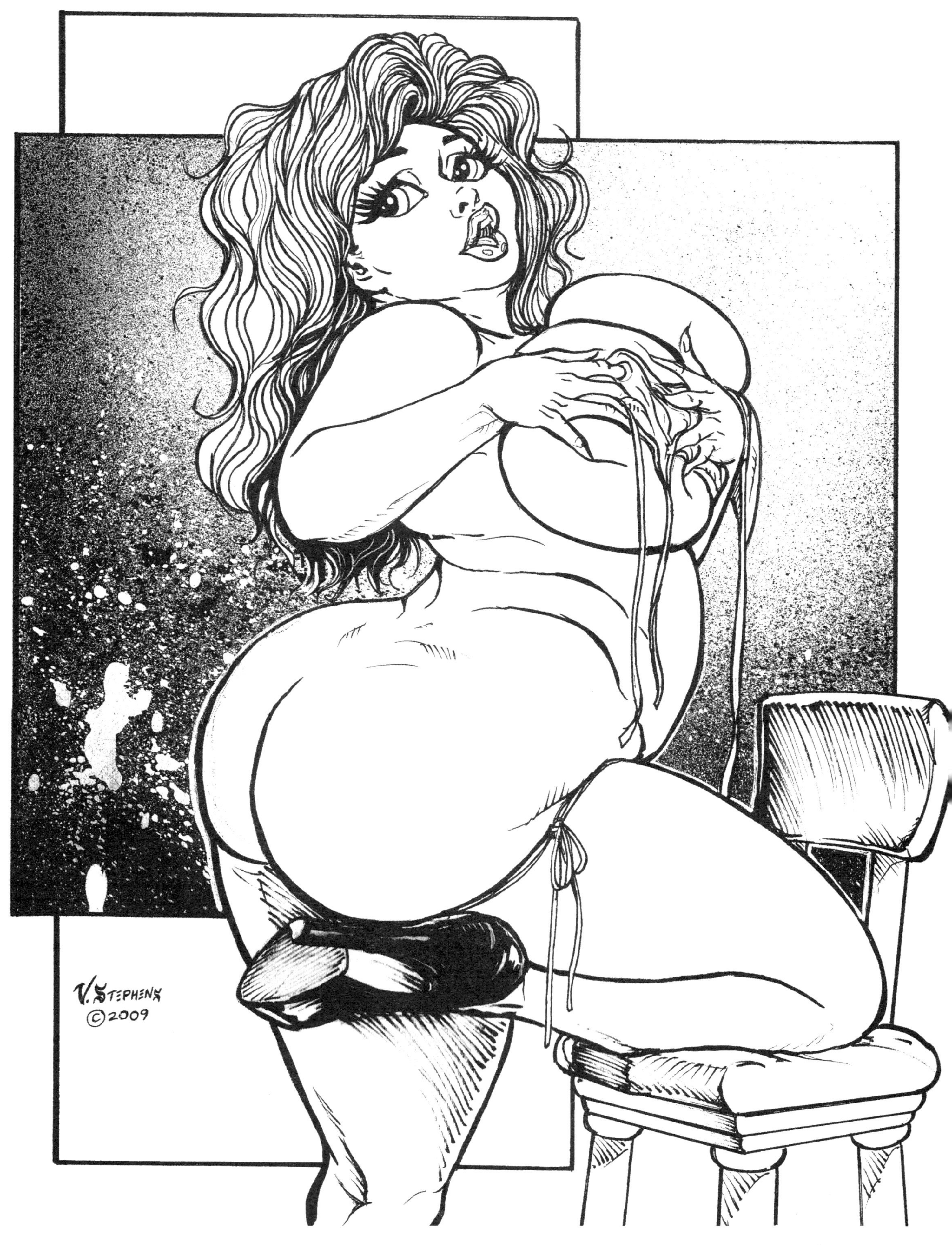
V. Stephens
©2009

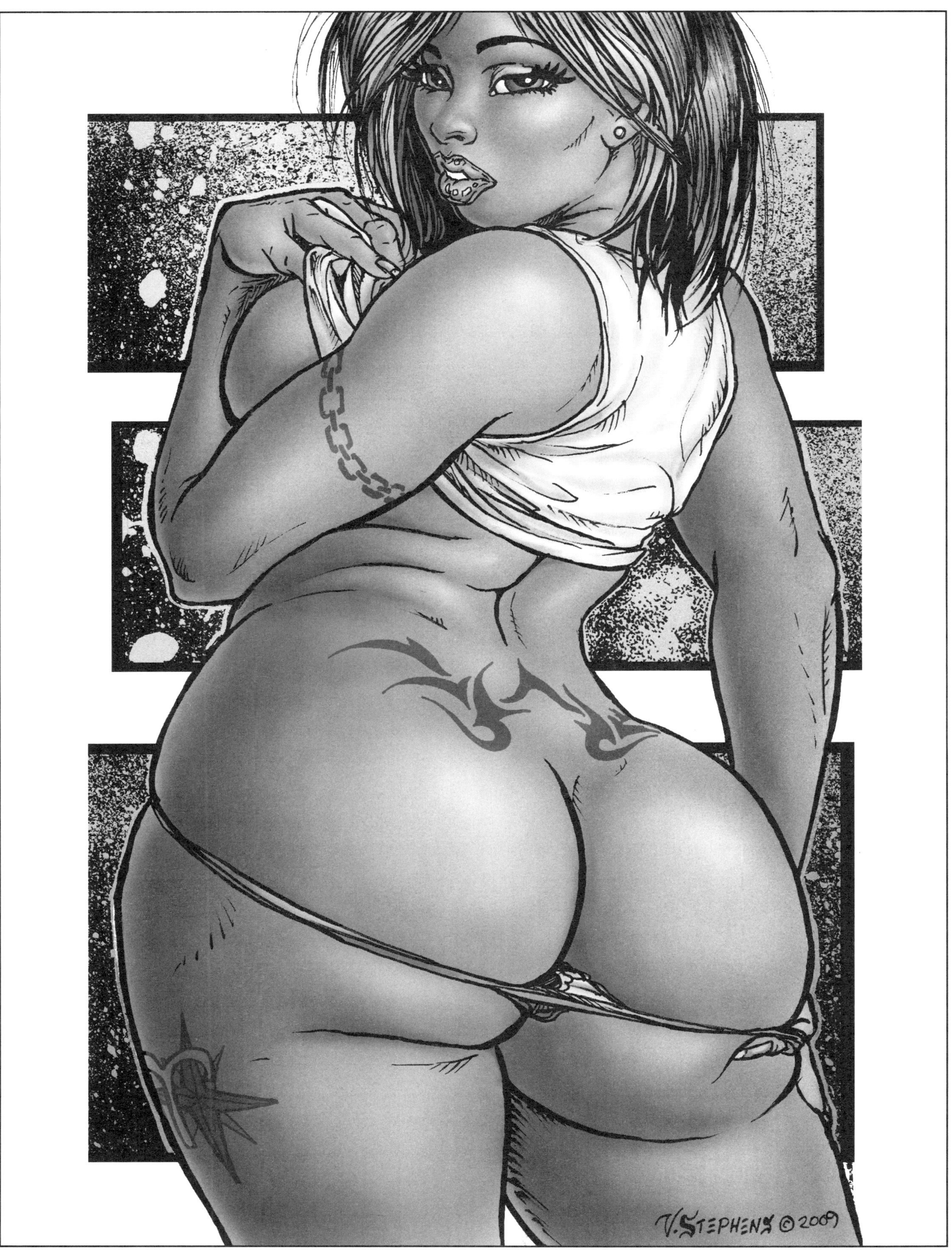
V. STEPHENS ©2009

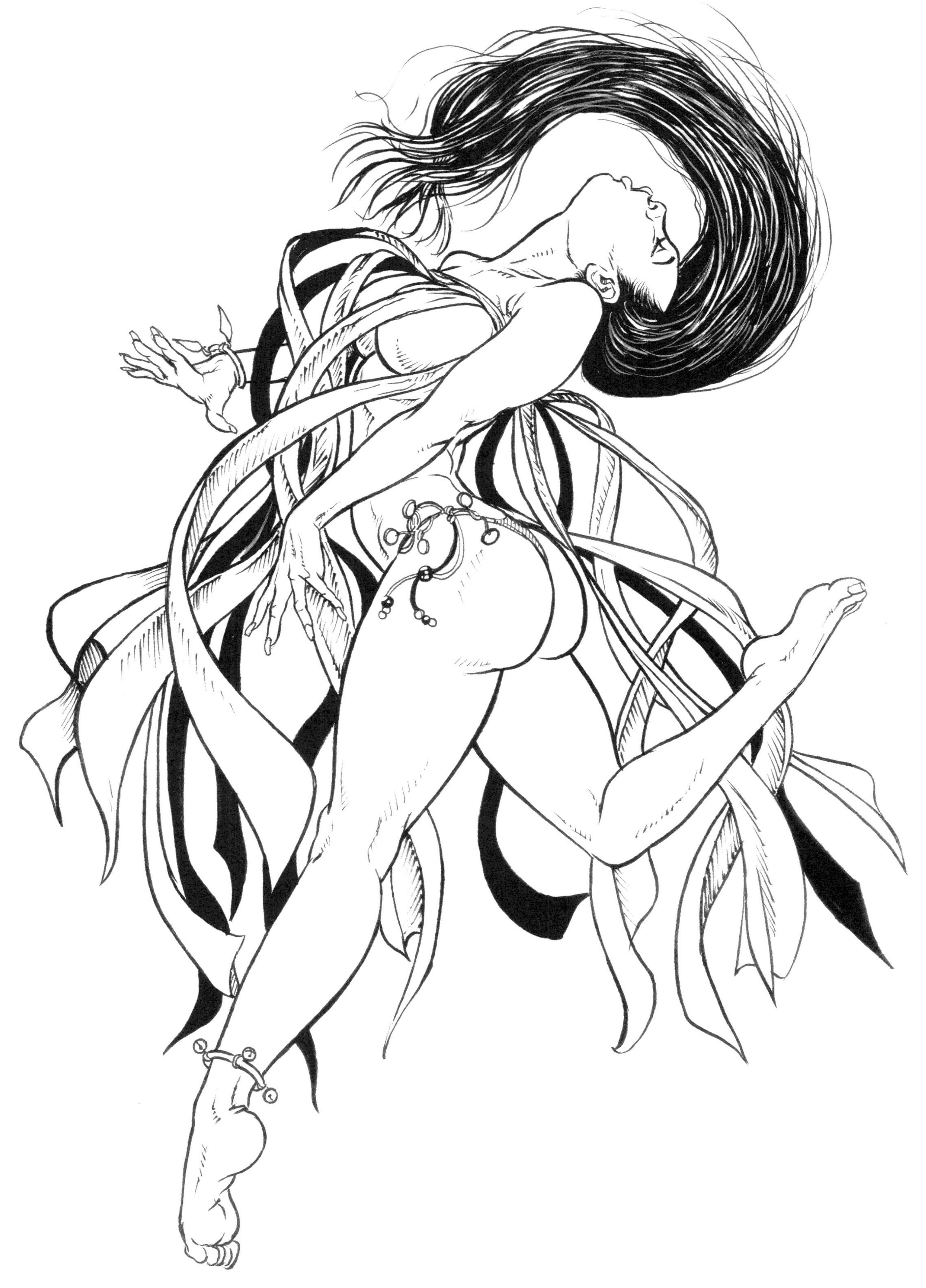

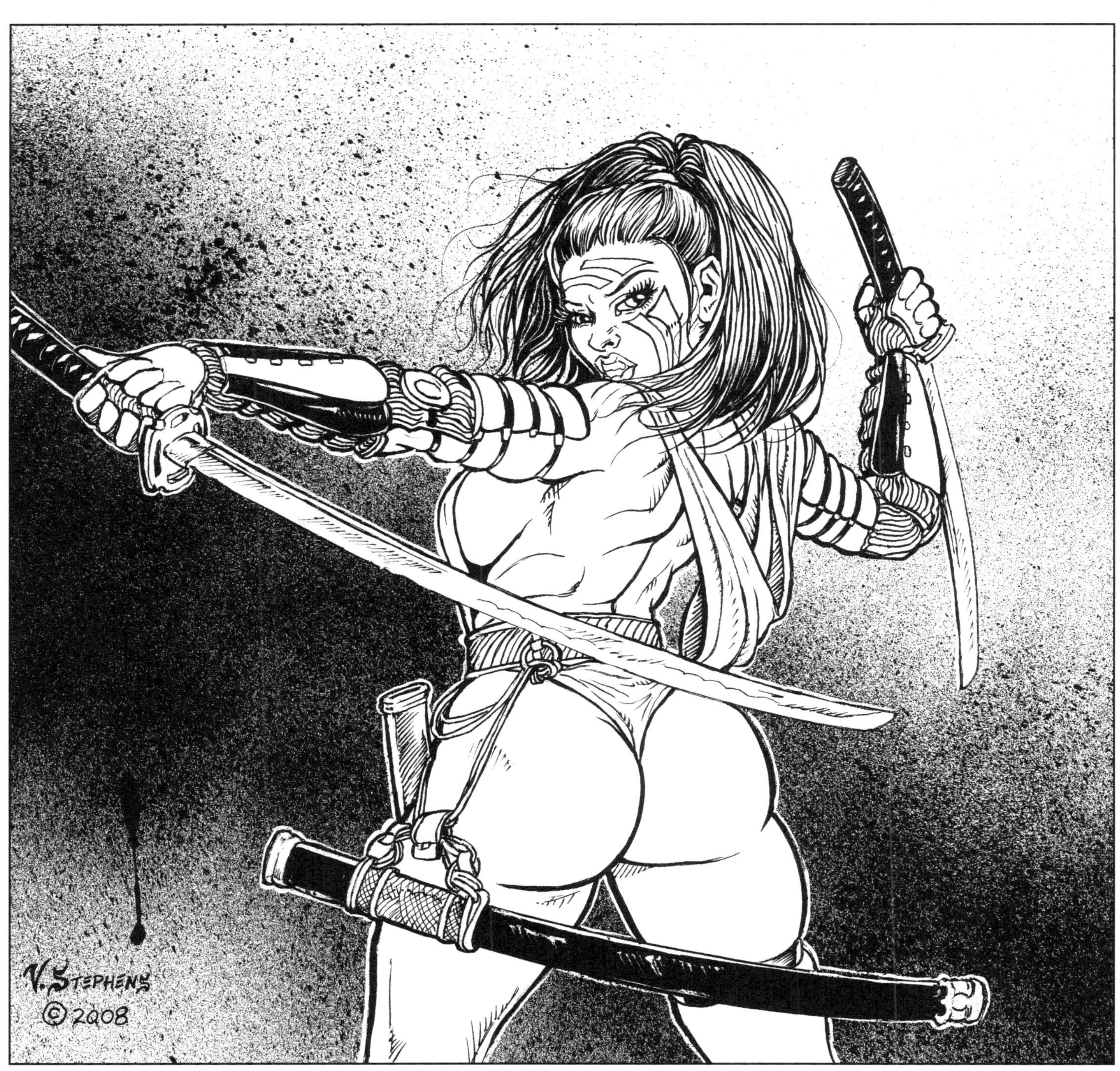
V. STEPHENS
©2008

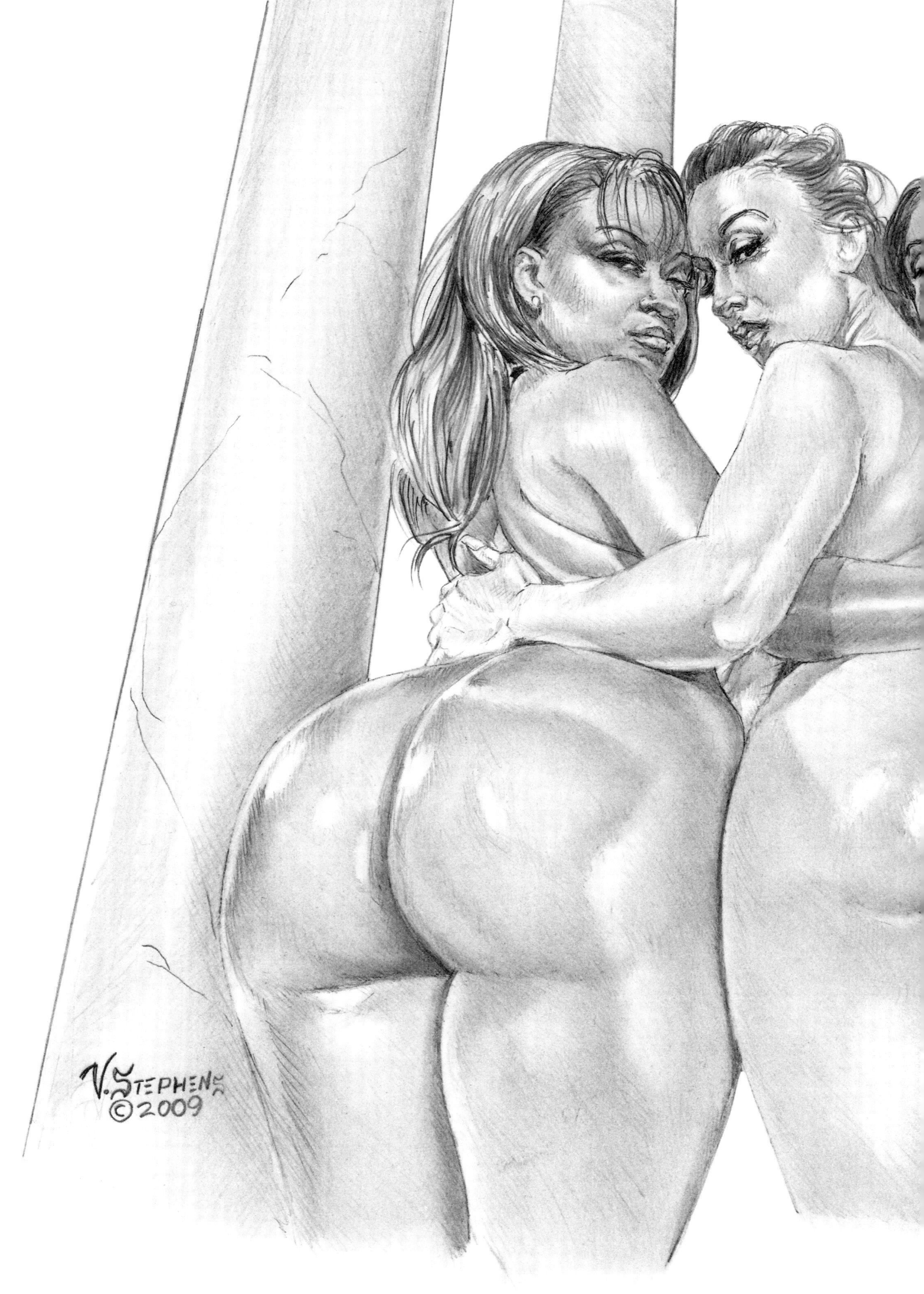
V. STEPHENS
©2009

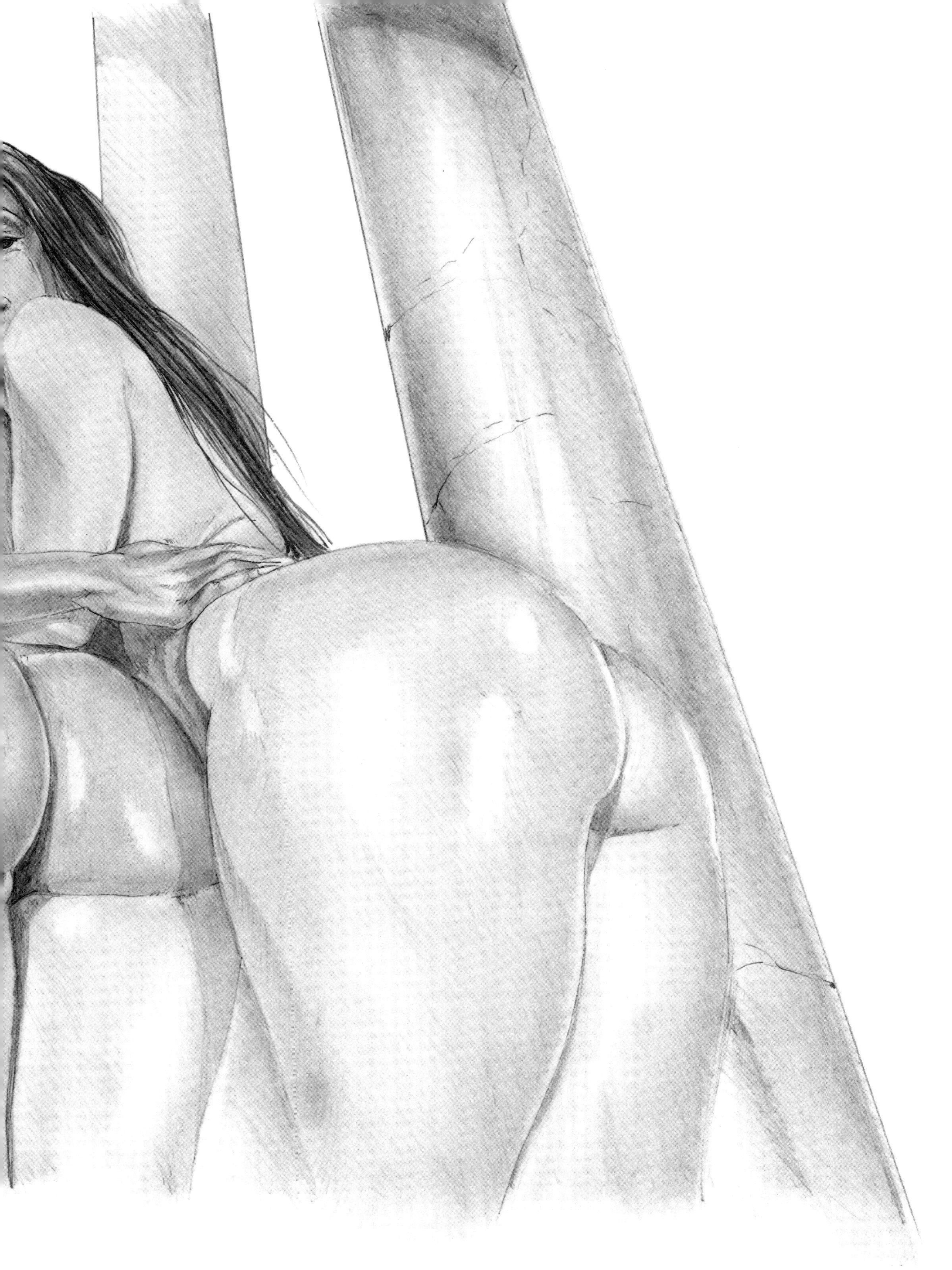

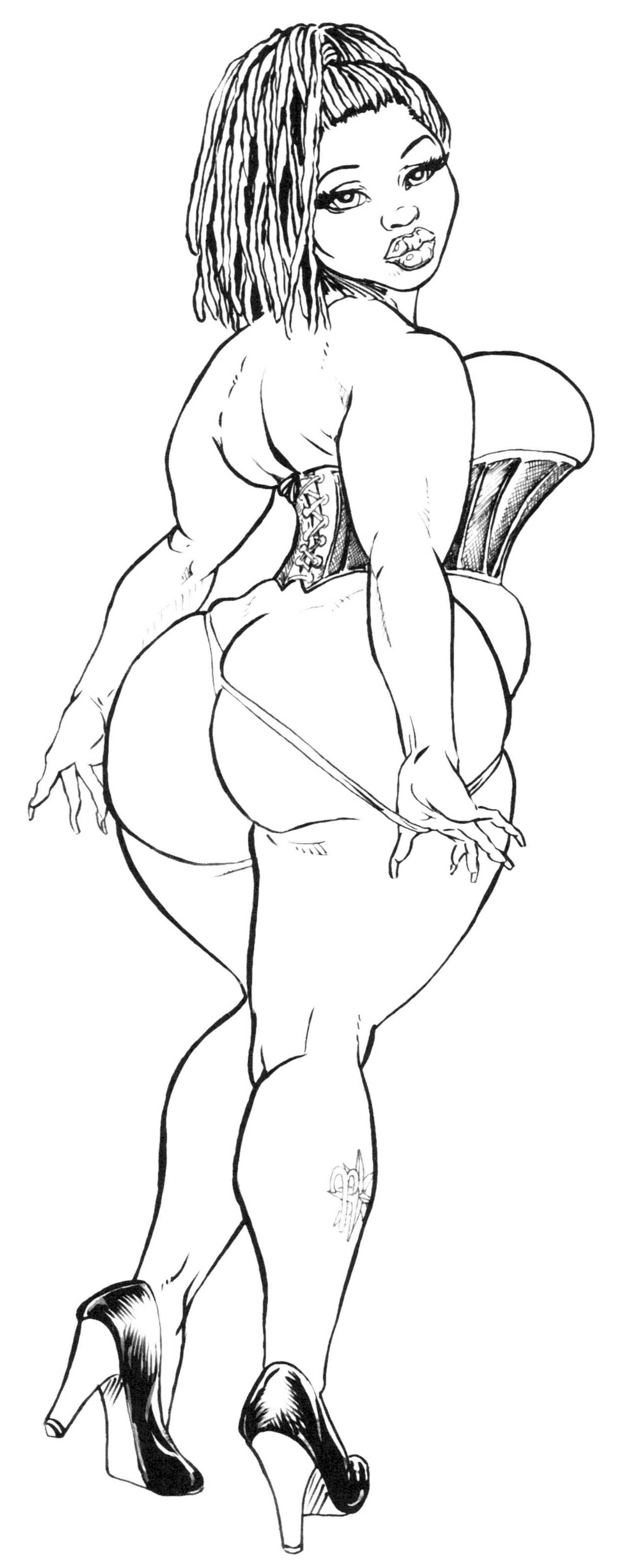

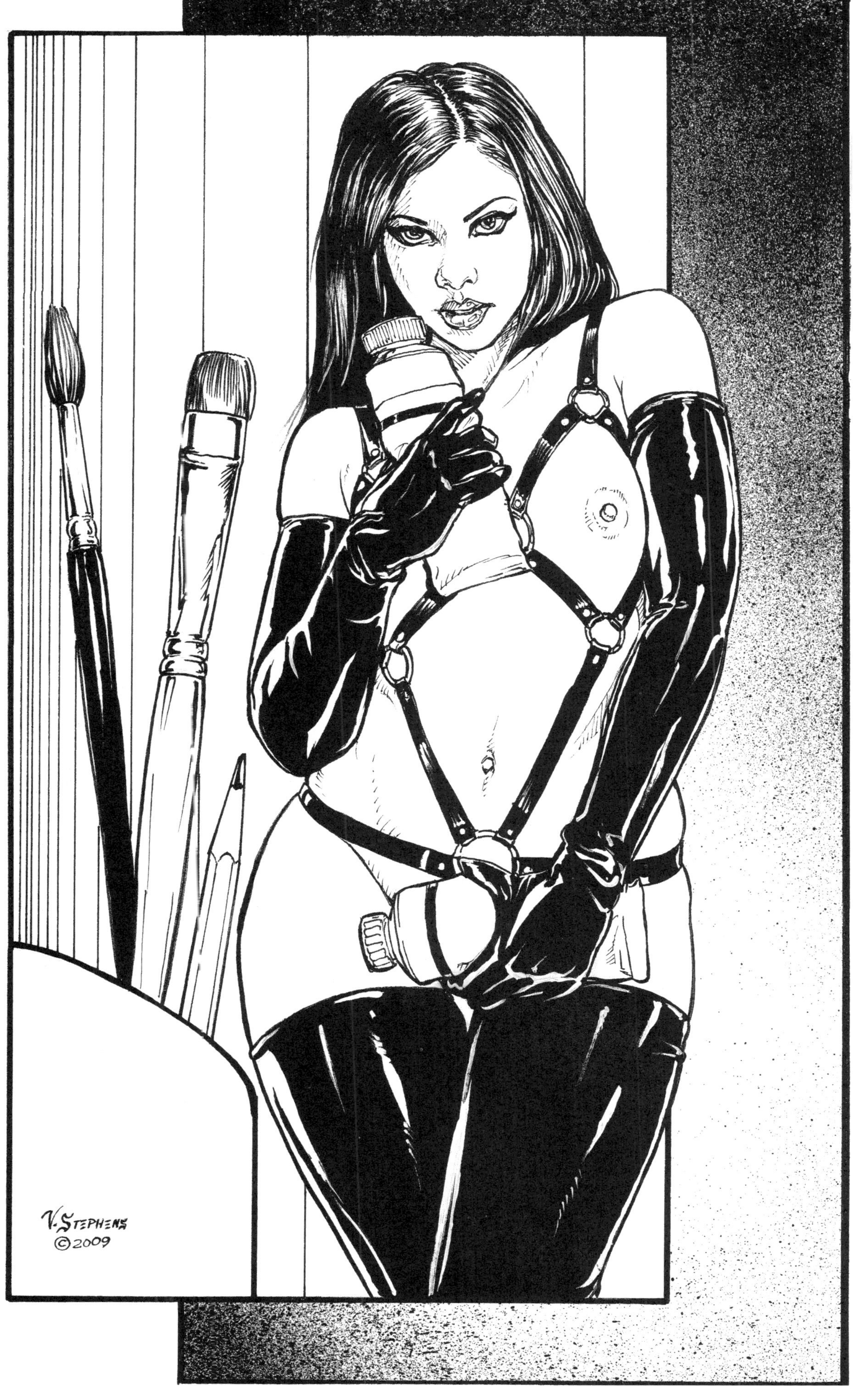
V. STEPHENS
©2009

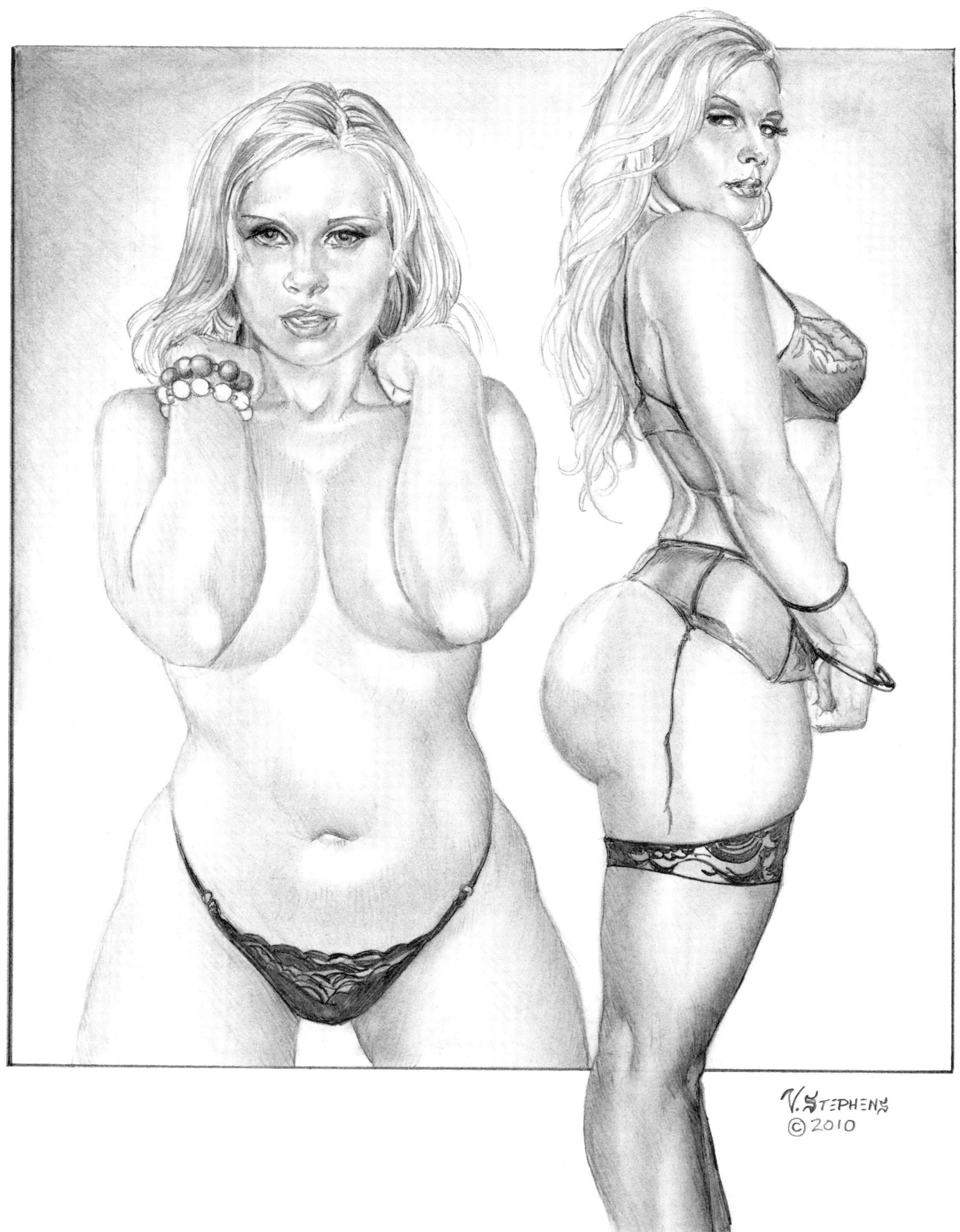
V. STEPHENS
©2010

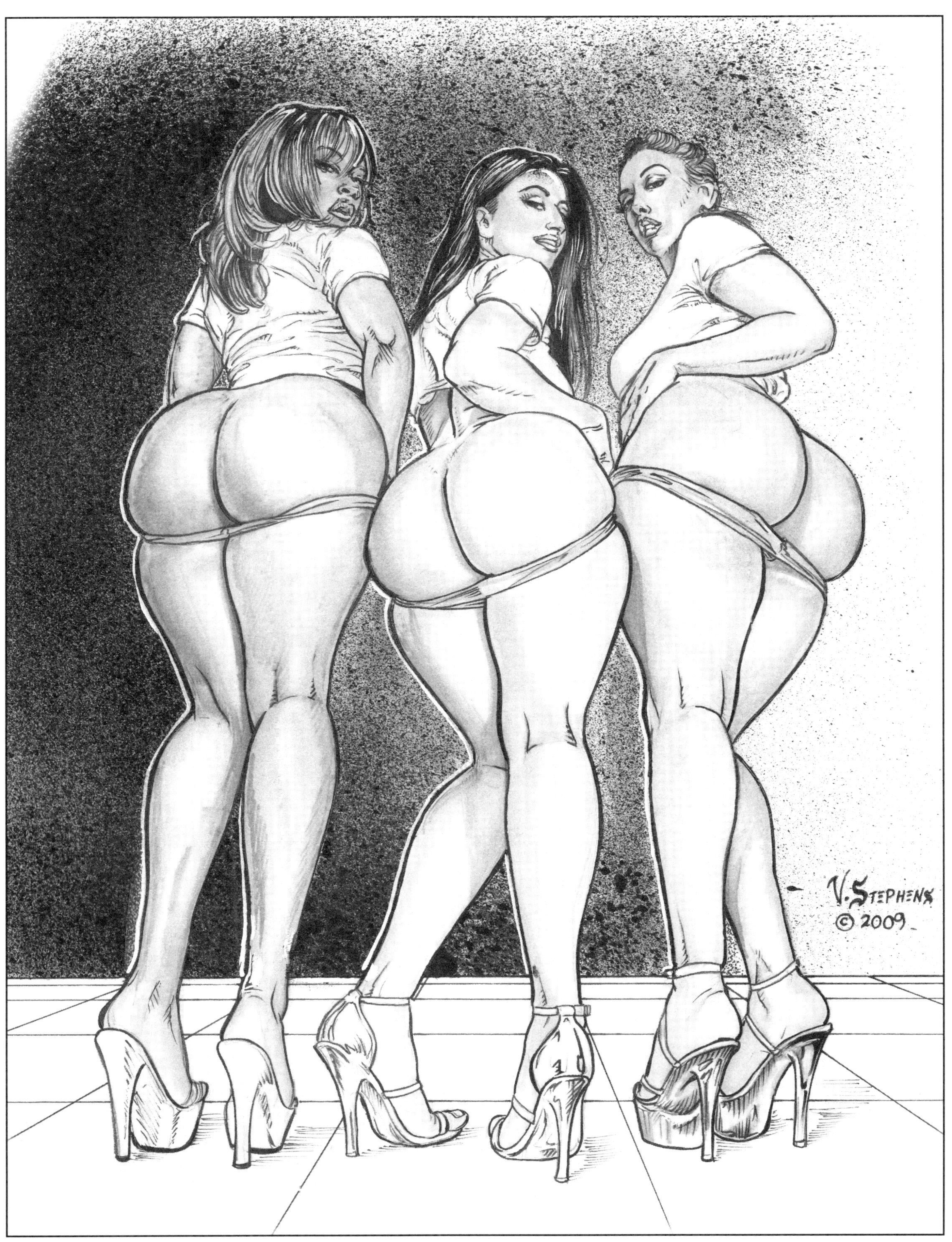
V. STEPHENS
© 2009

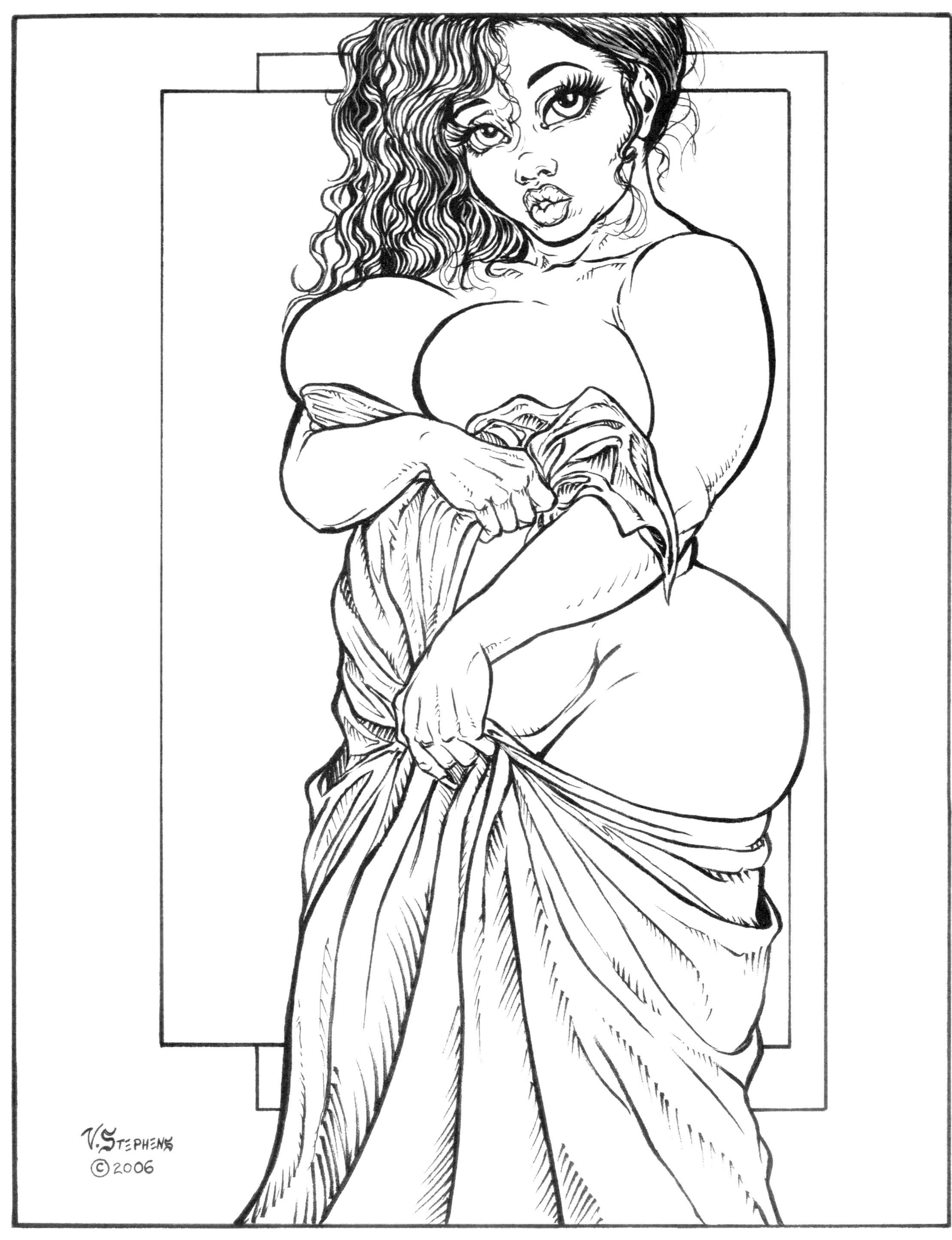
V.Stephens
©2006

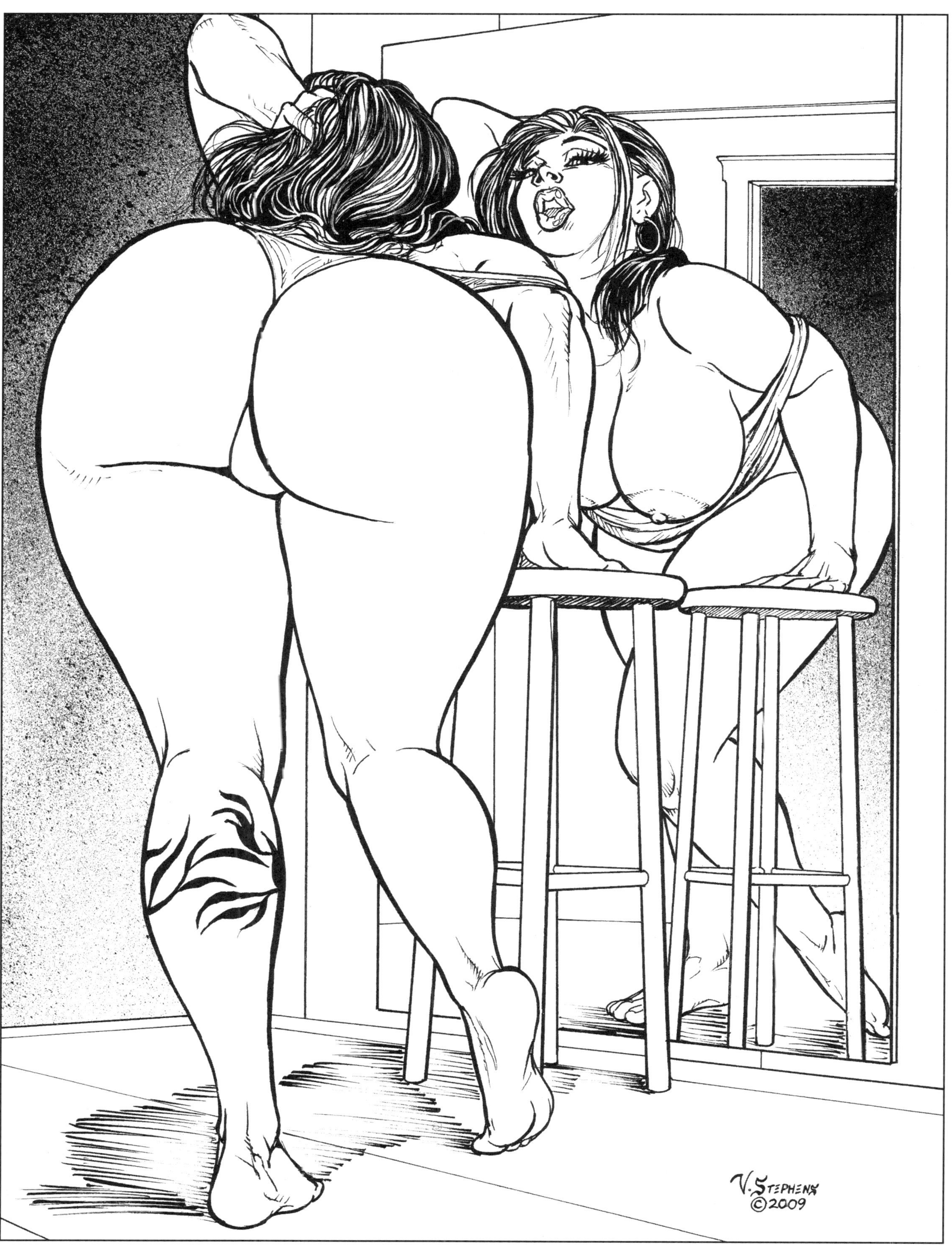
V. Stephens
©2009

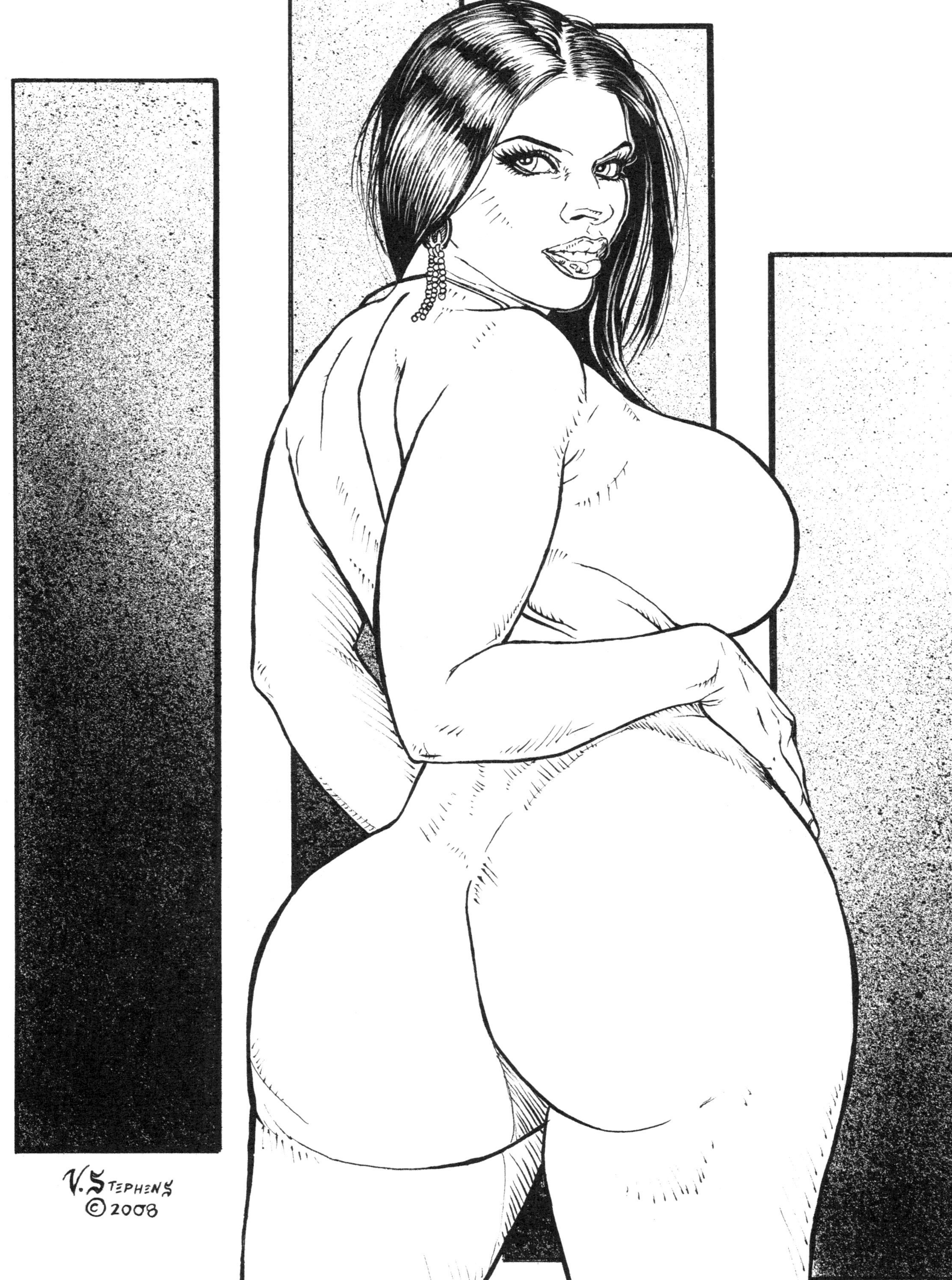
V. Stephens
©2008

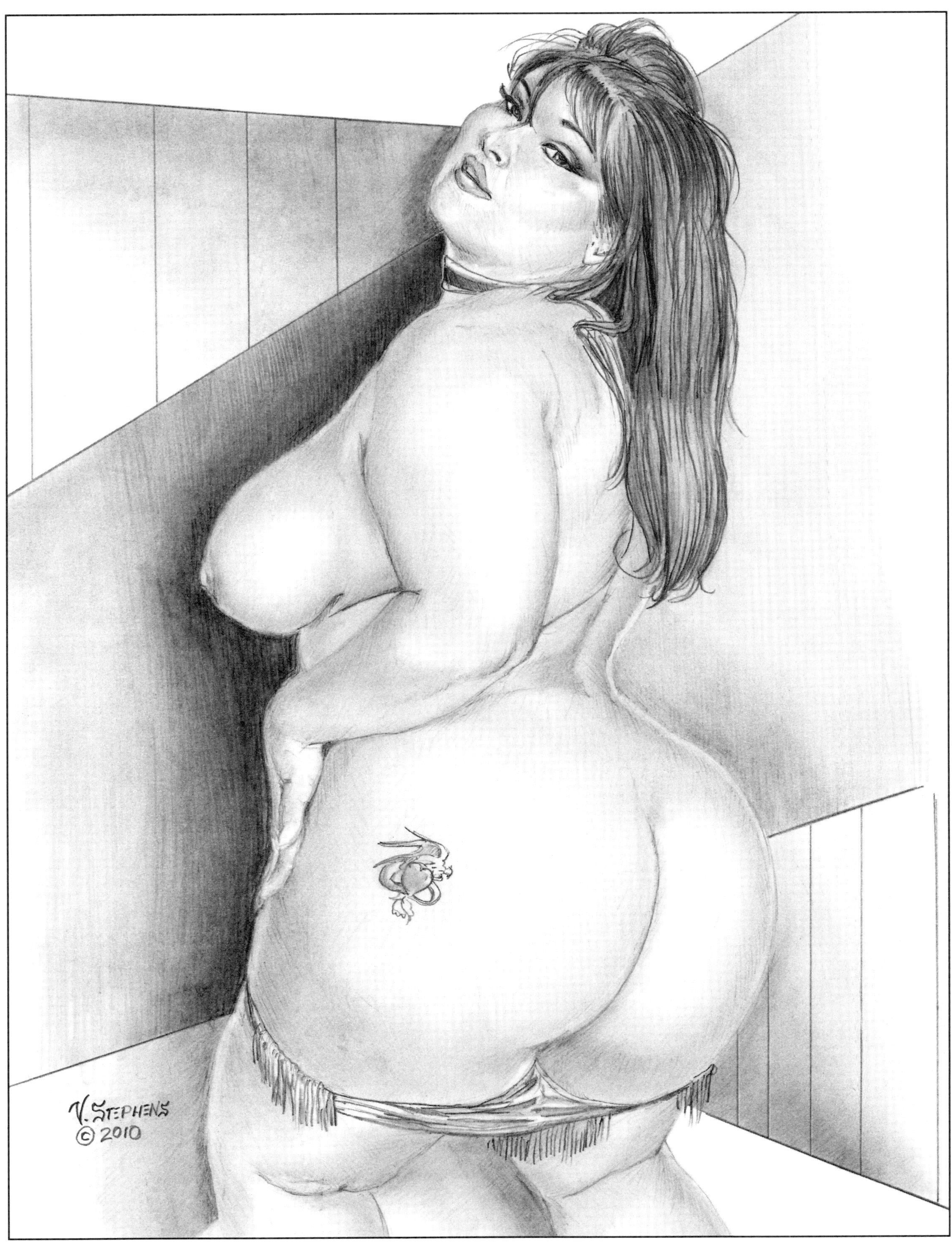
V. STEPHENS
© 2010

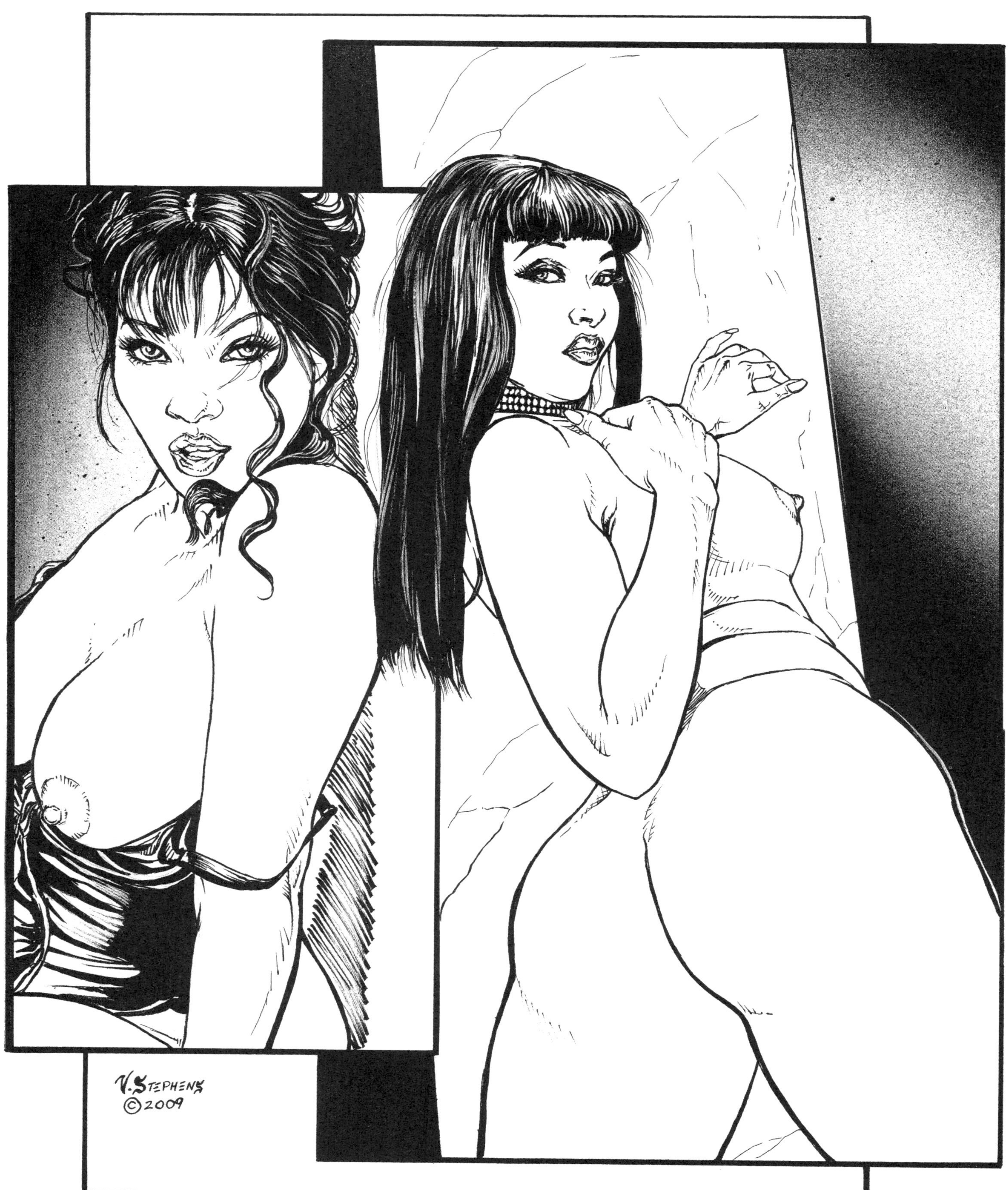
V. Stephens
©2009

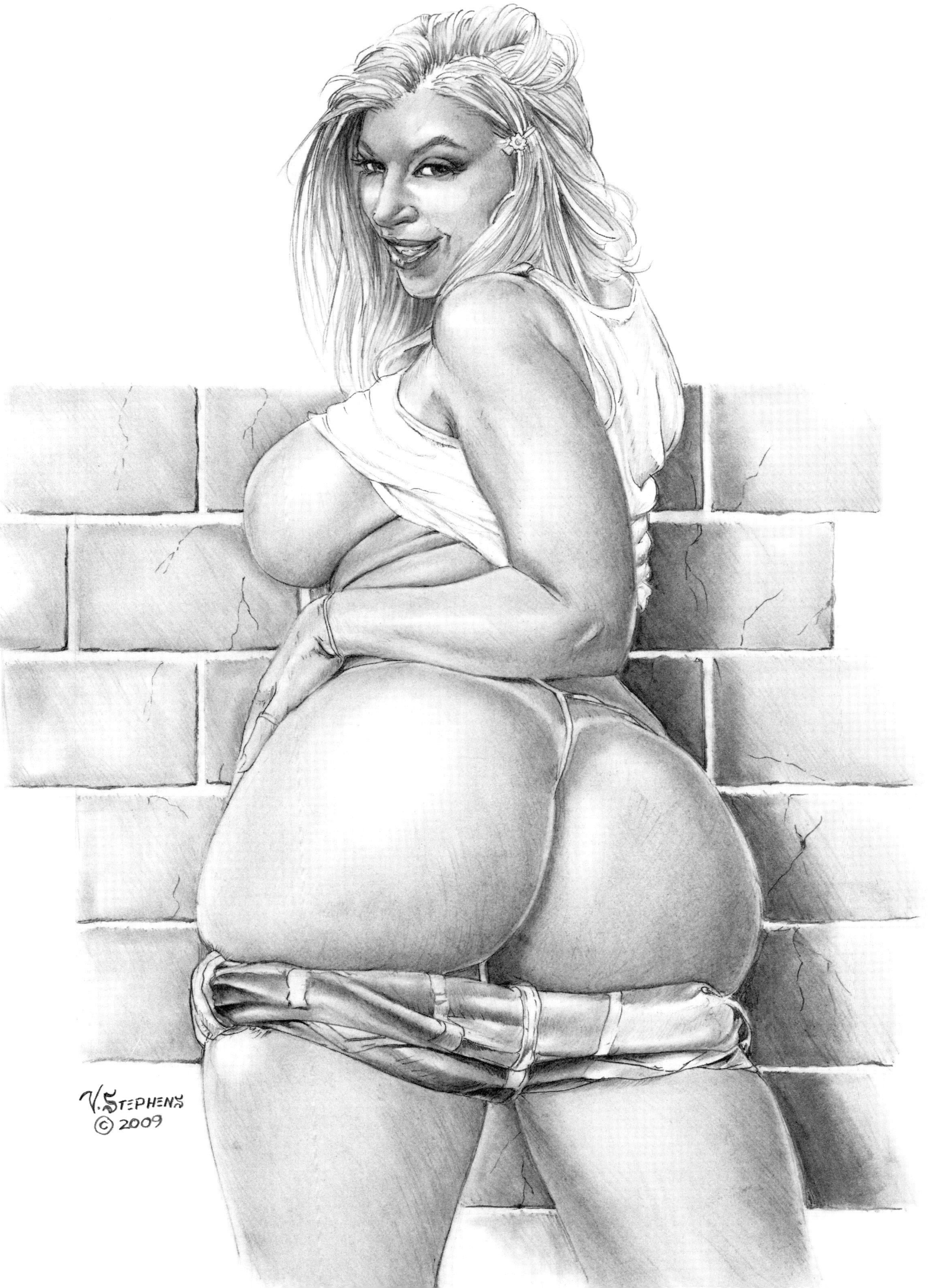
V. STEPHENS
© 2009

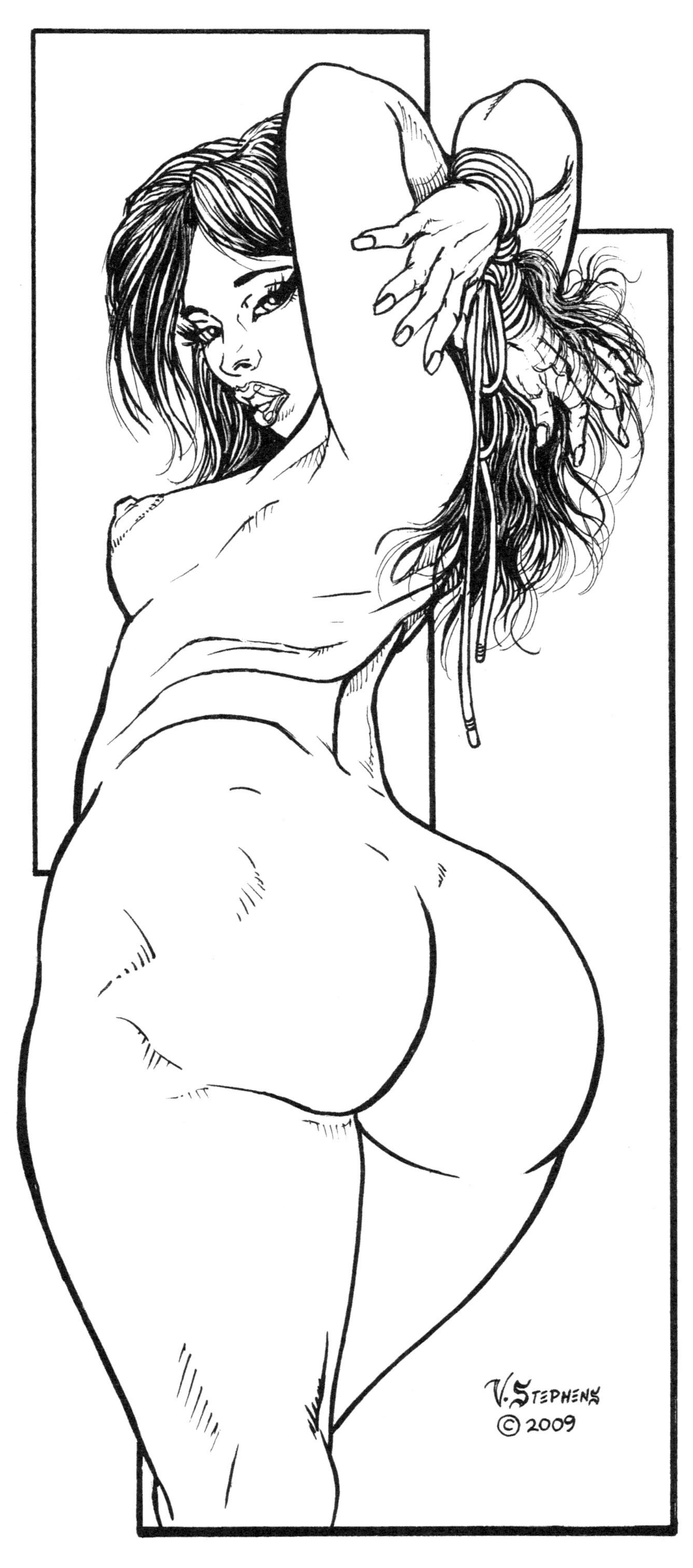
V. Stephens
© 2009

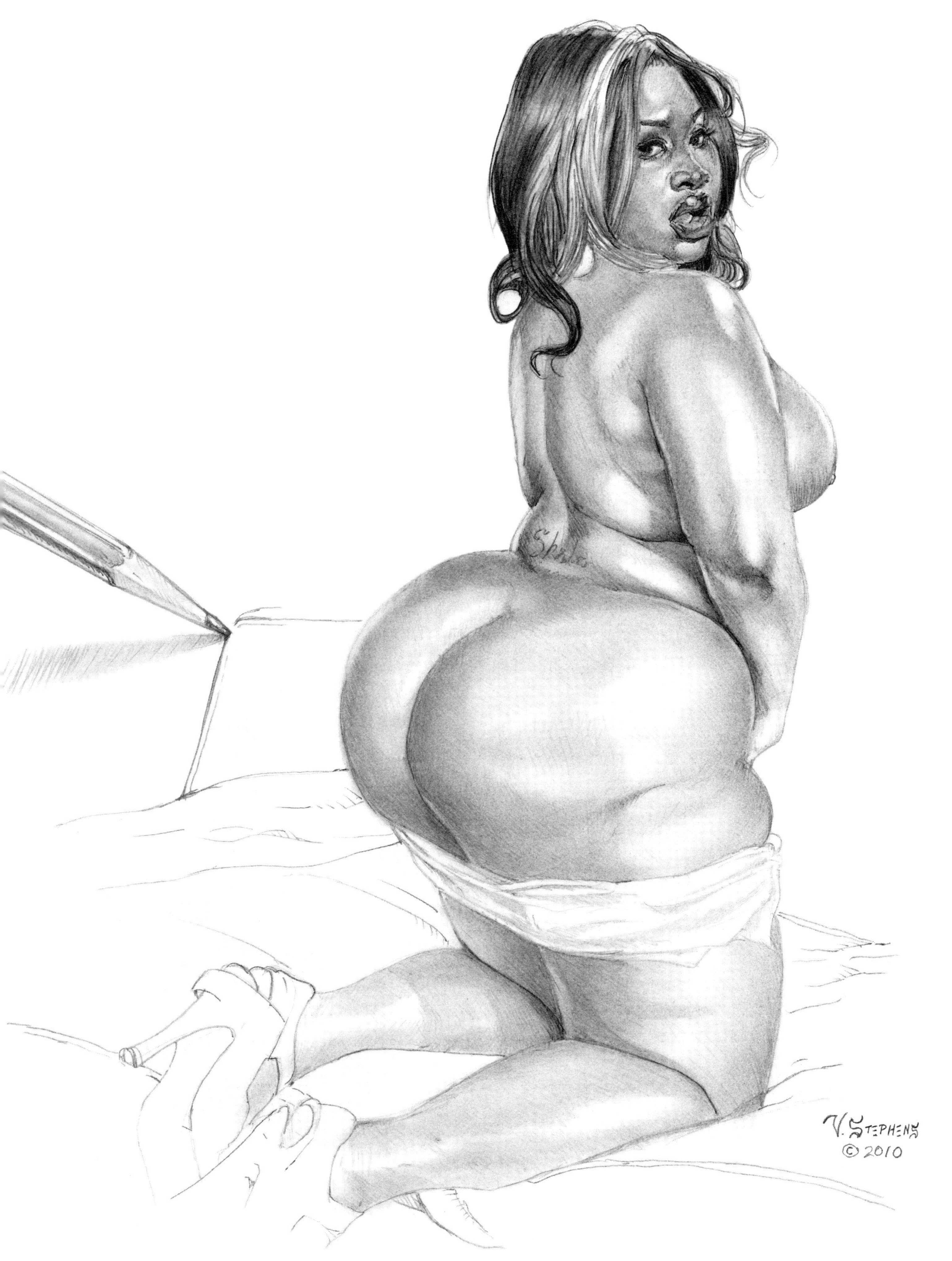
V. STEPHENS
© 2010

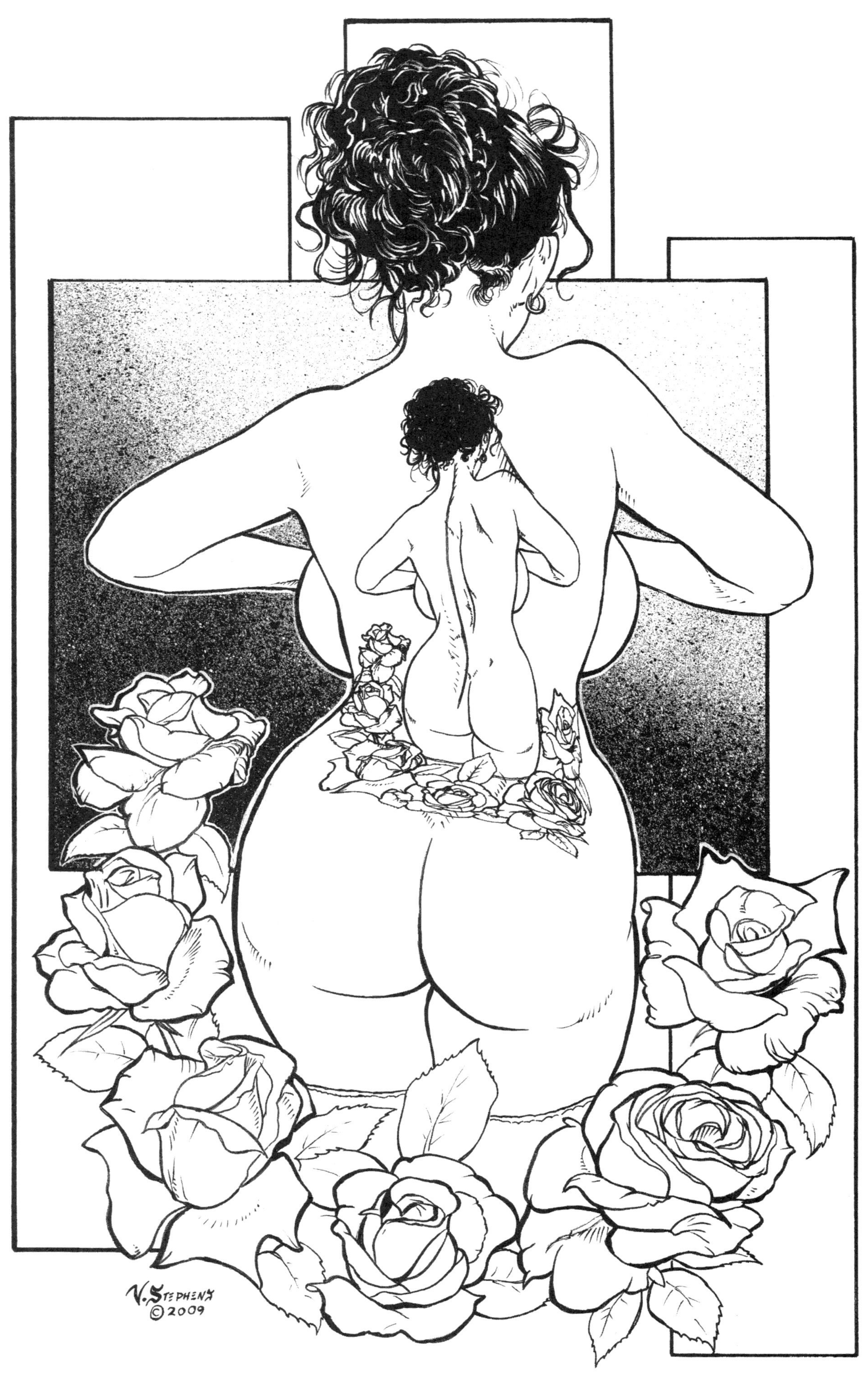
V. STEPHENY
©2009

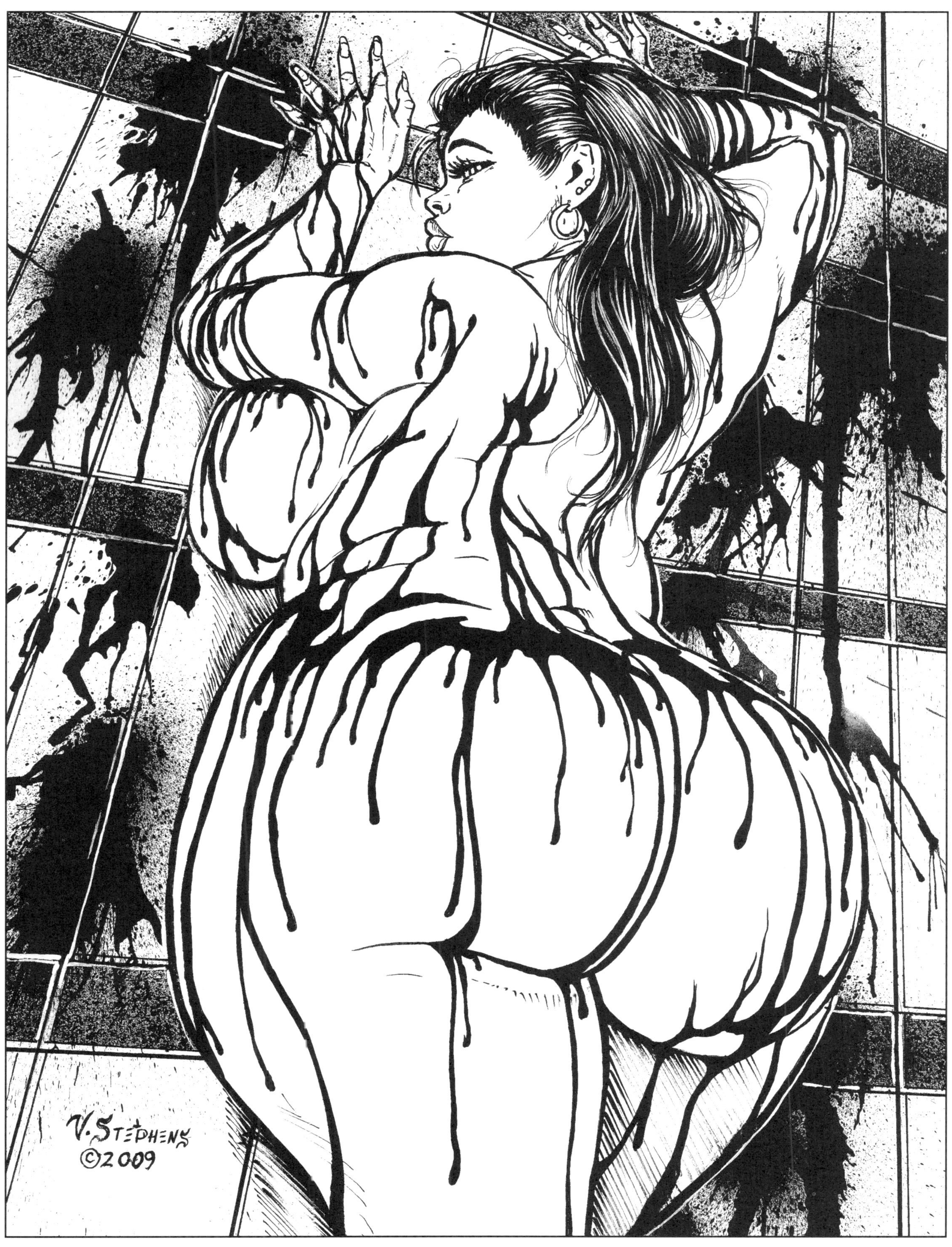
V. STEPHENS
©2009

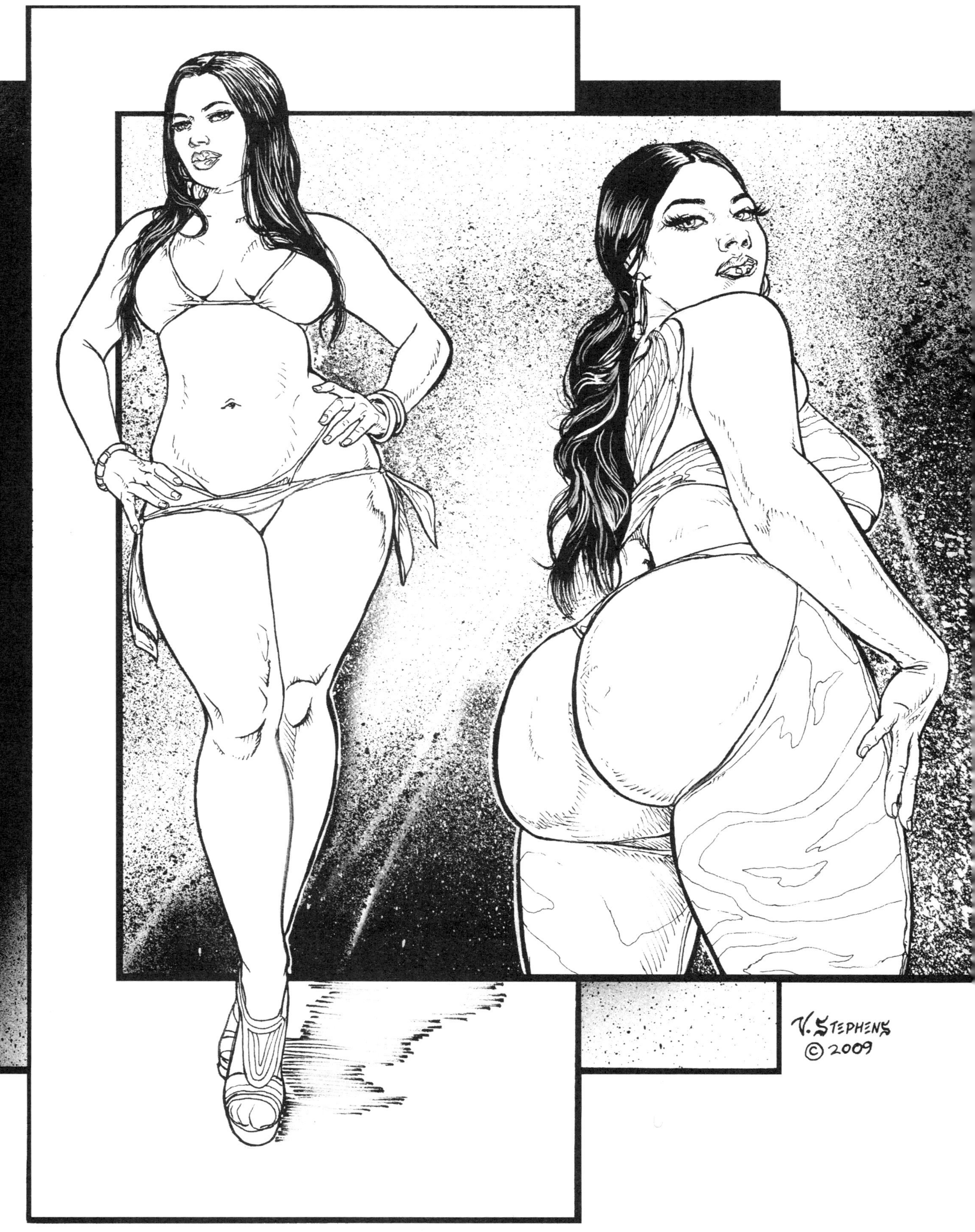
V. STEPHENS
© 2009

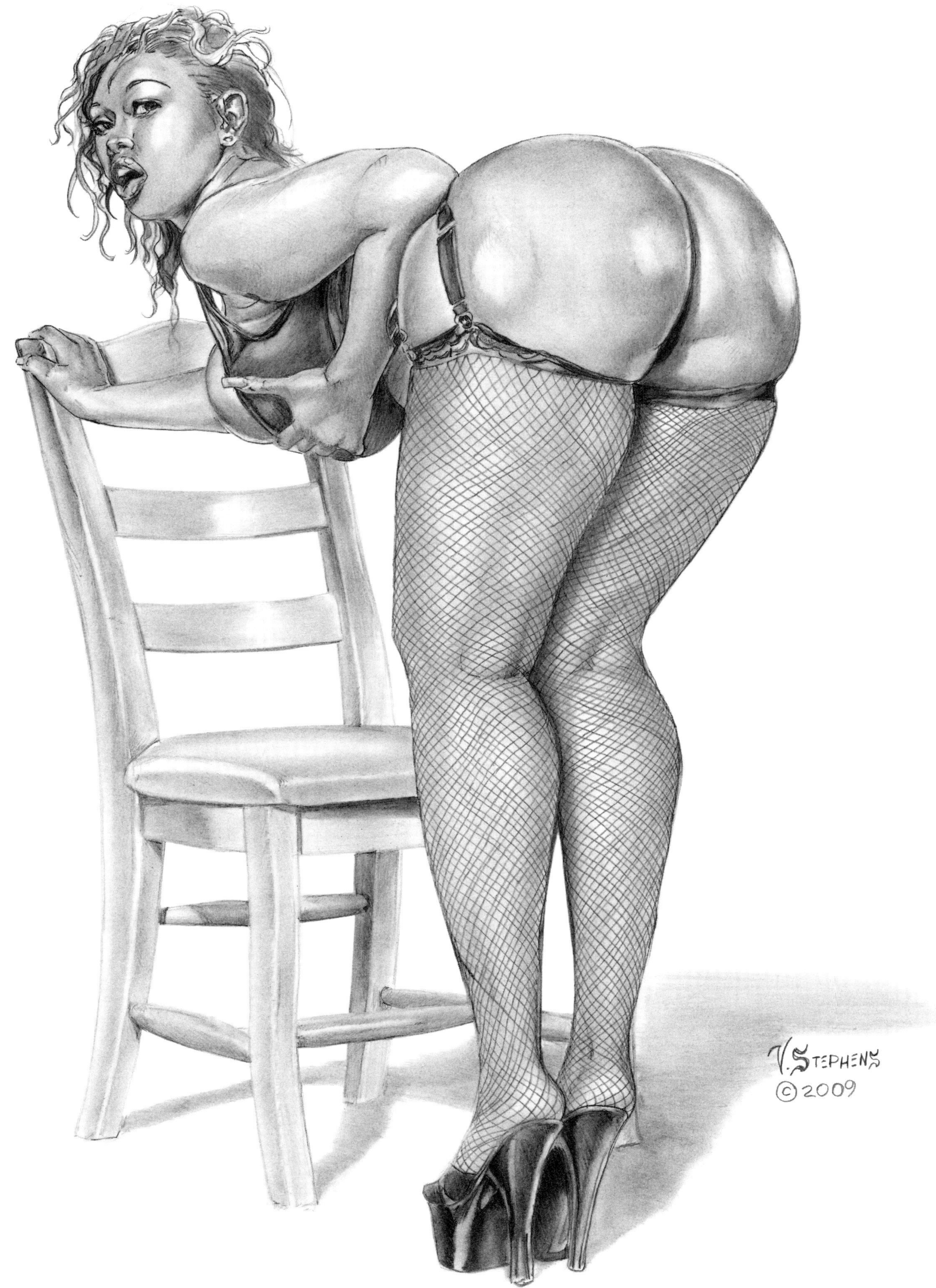
V. STEPHENS
©2009

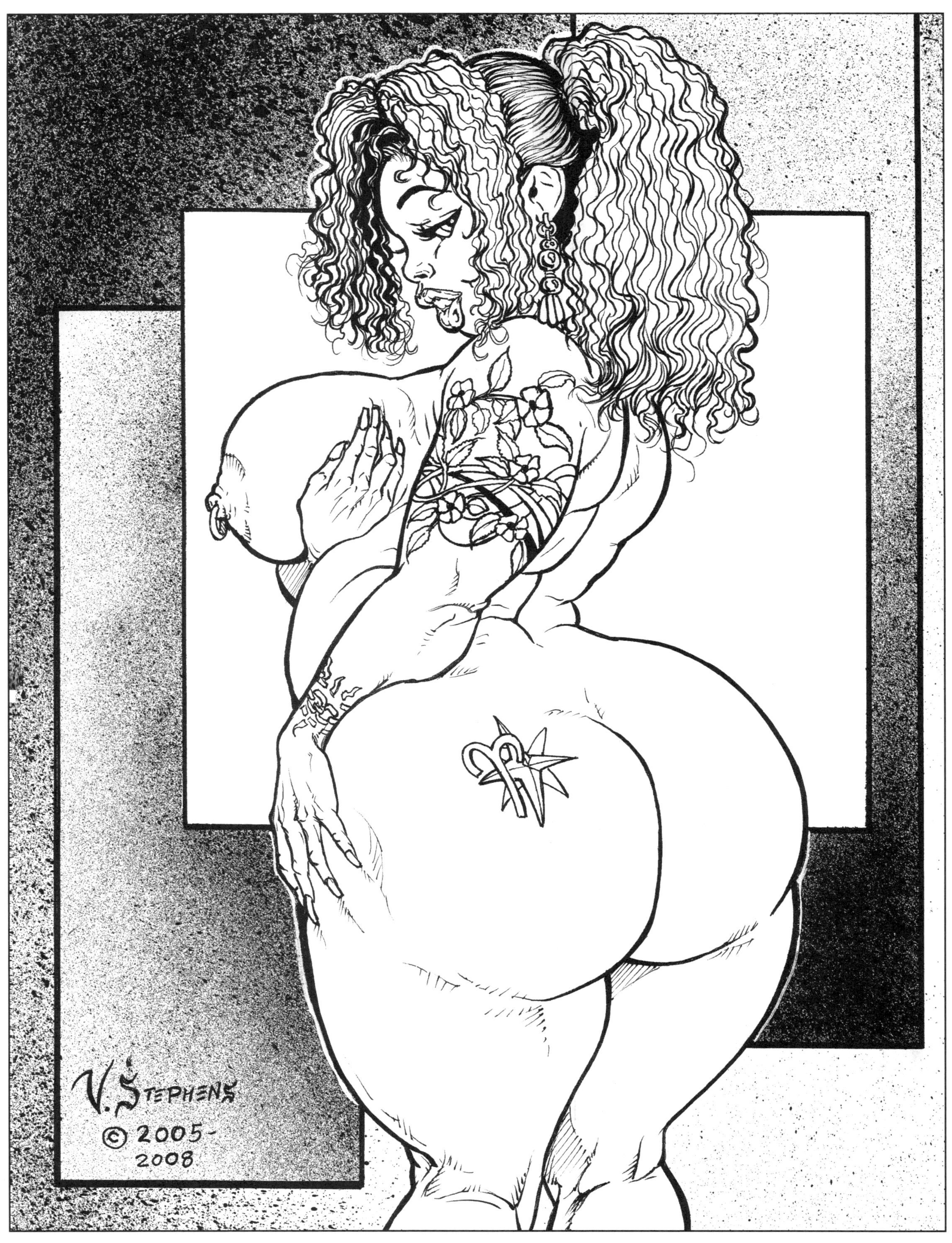
V. Stephens
© 2005-
2008

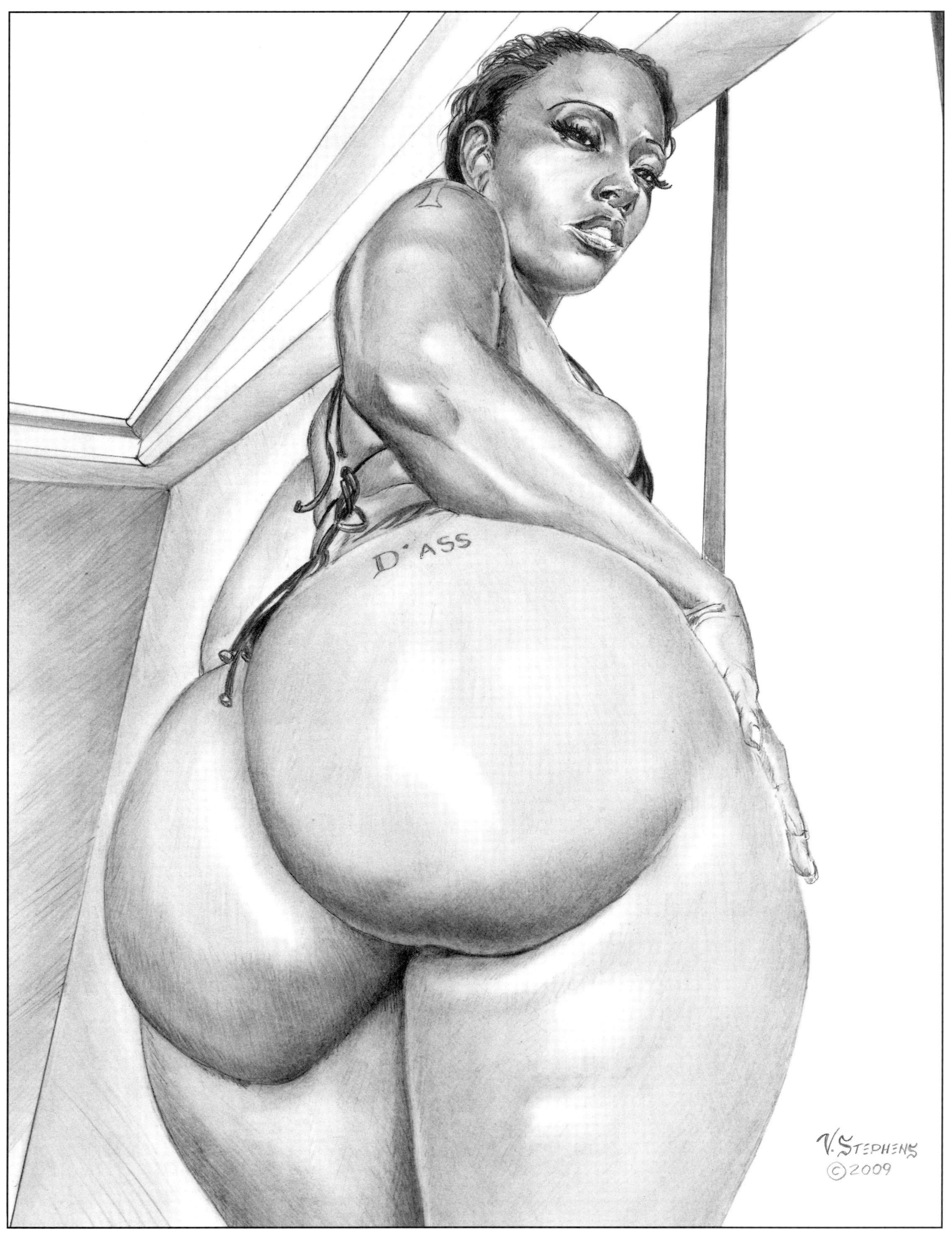
D'ASS
V. STEPHENS
©2009

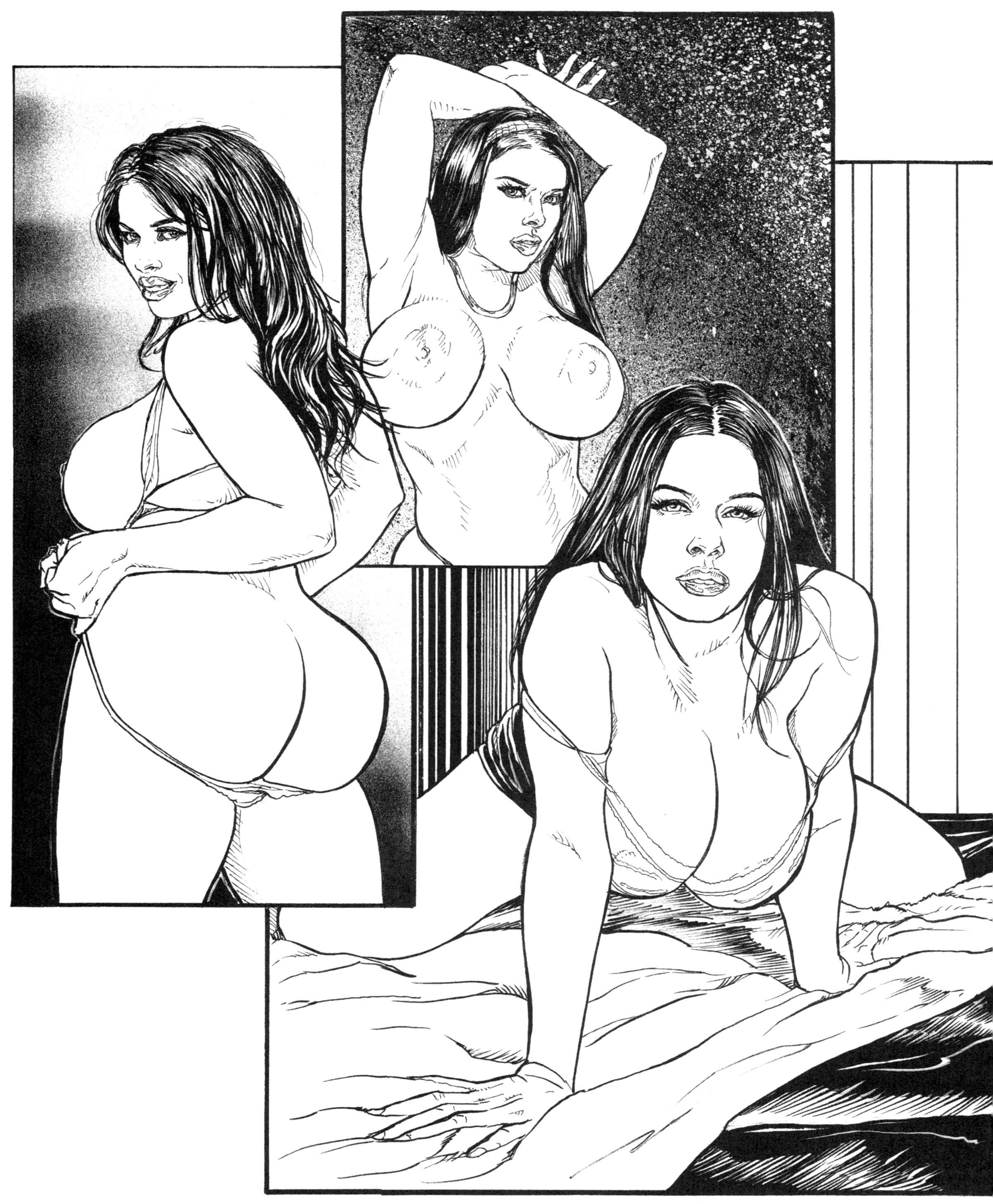

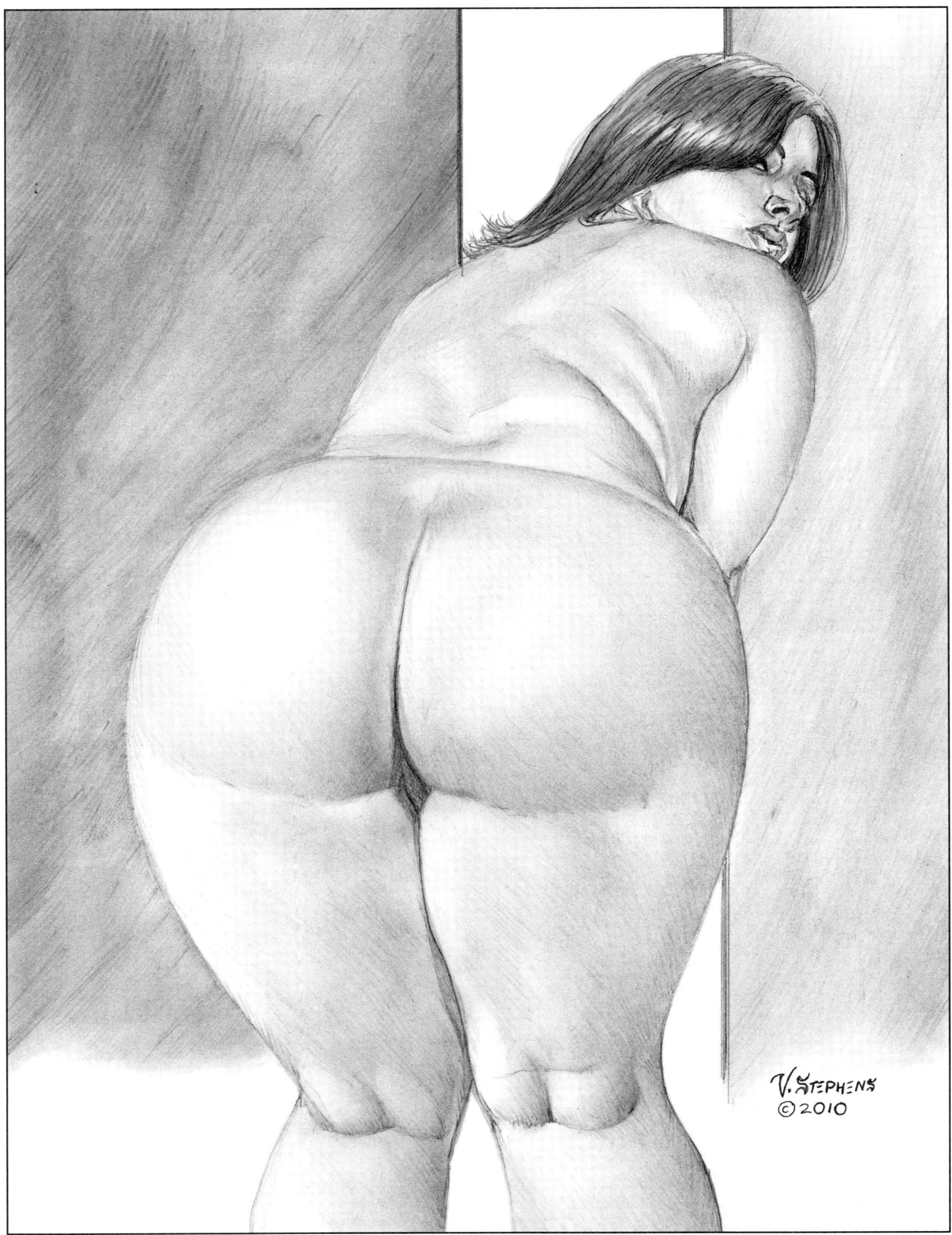
V. STEPHENS
©2010

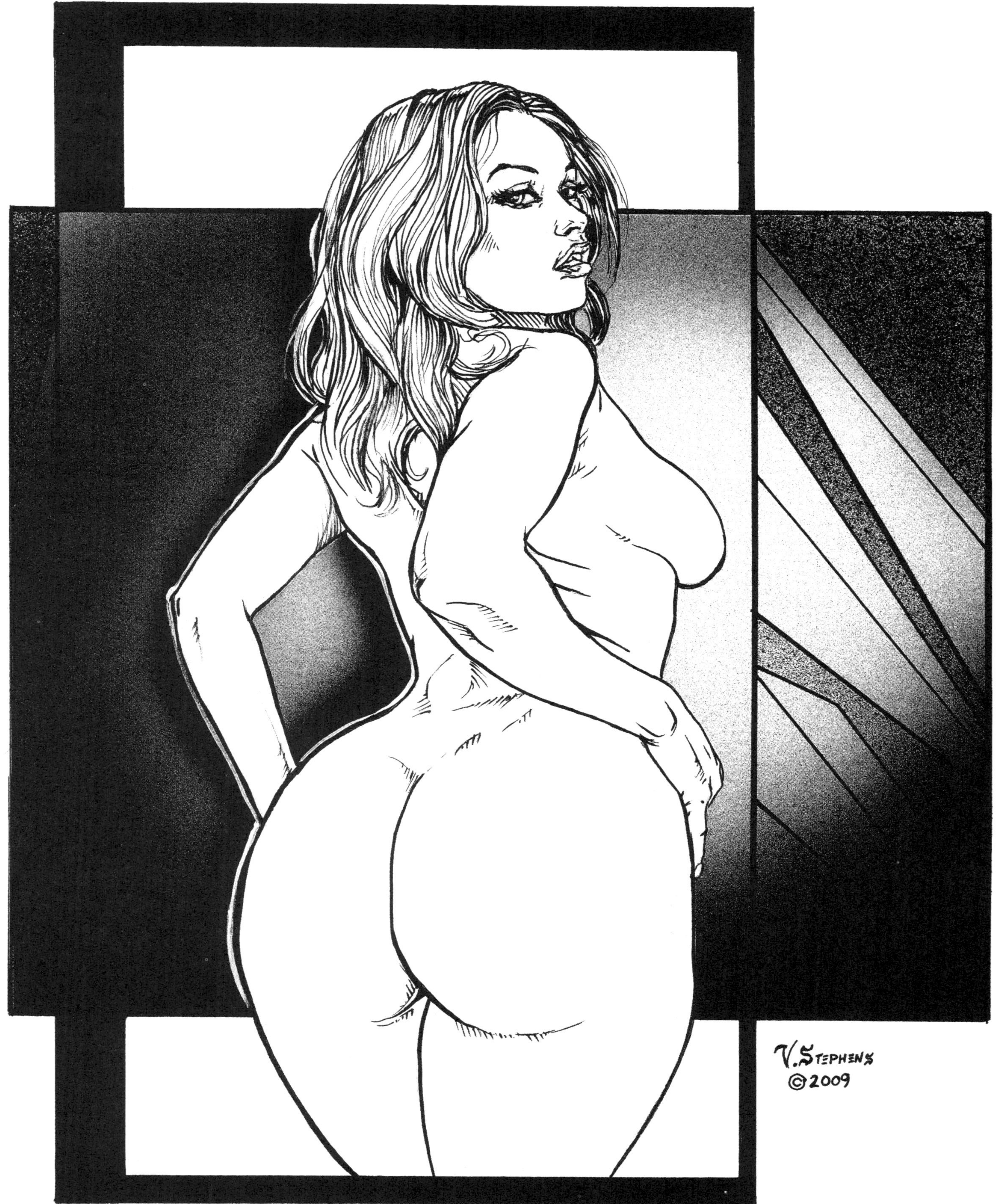
V.Stephens
©2009

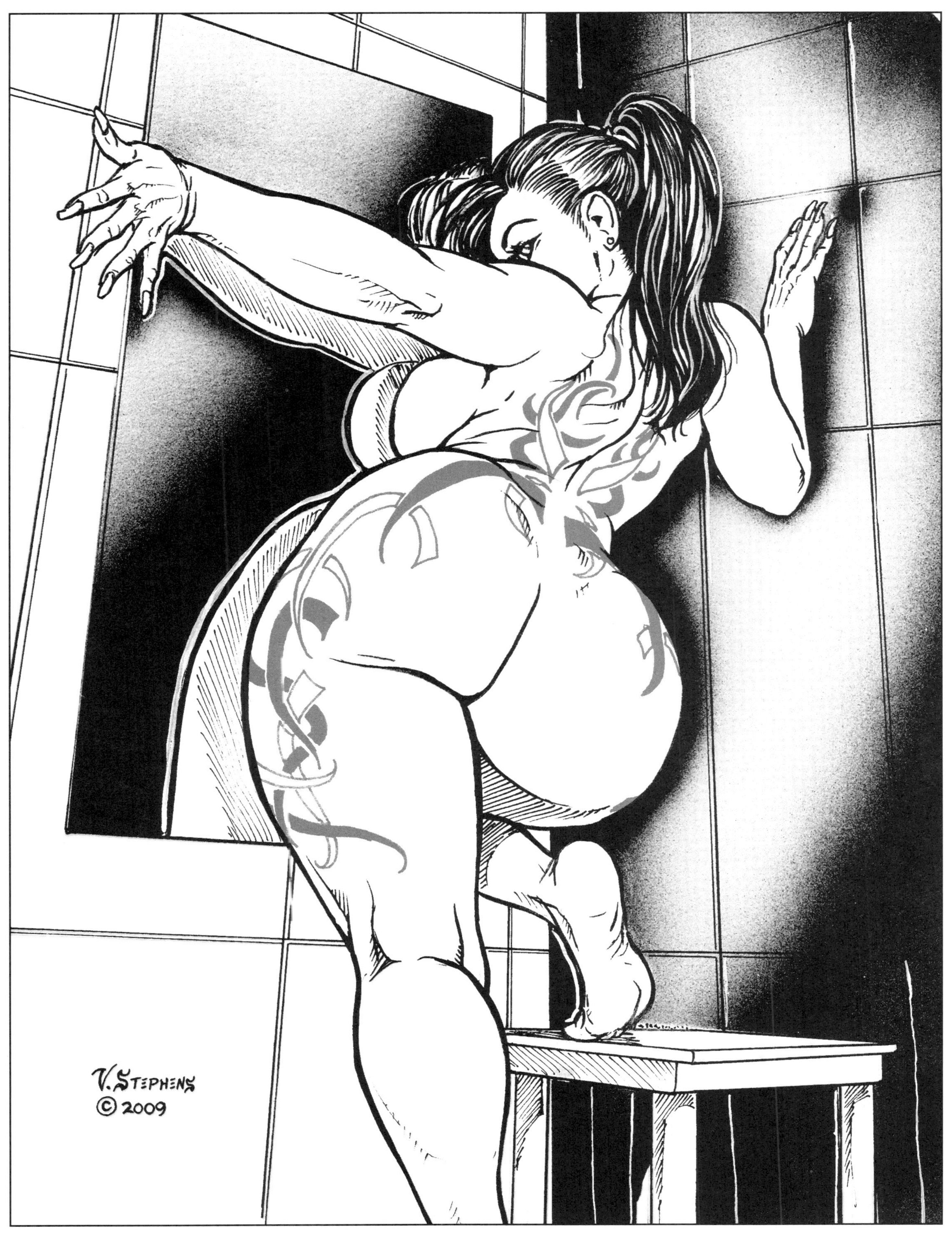
V. Stephens
© 2009

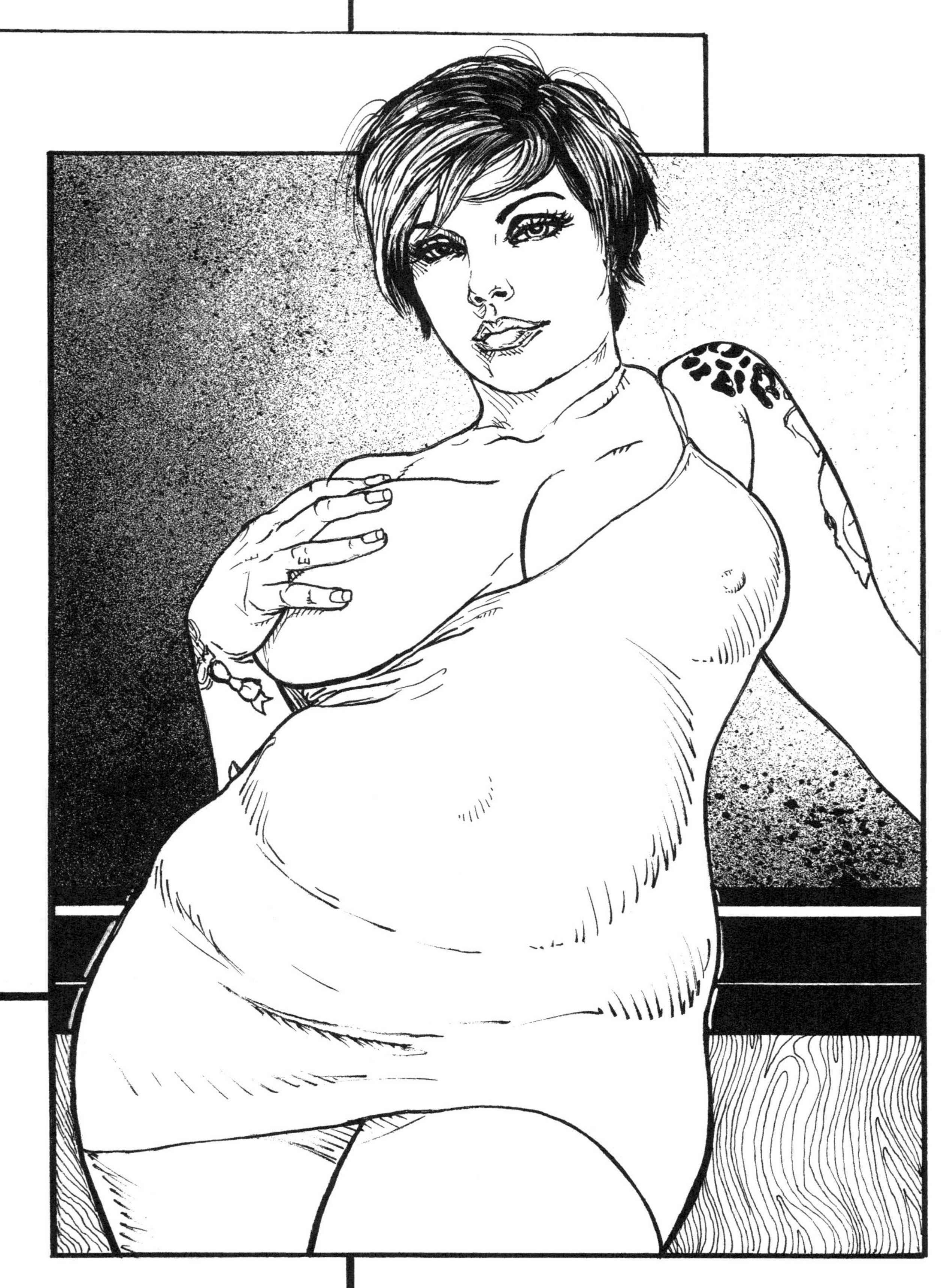

V. STEPHENS
©2009

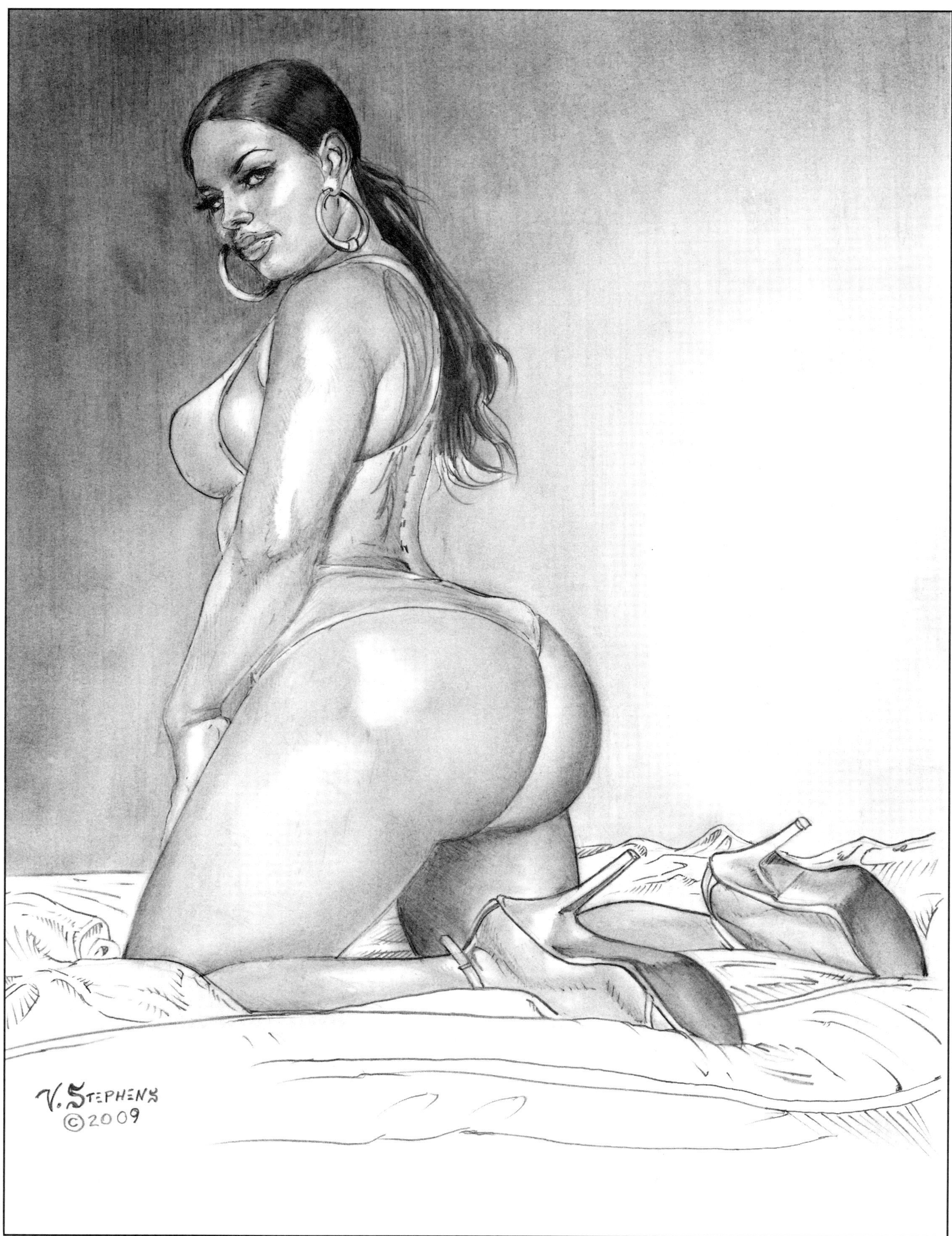
V. STEPHENS
©2009

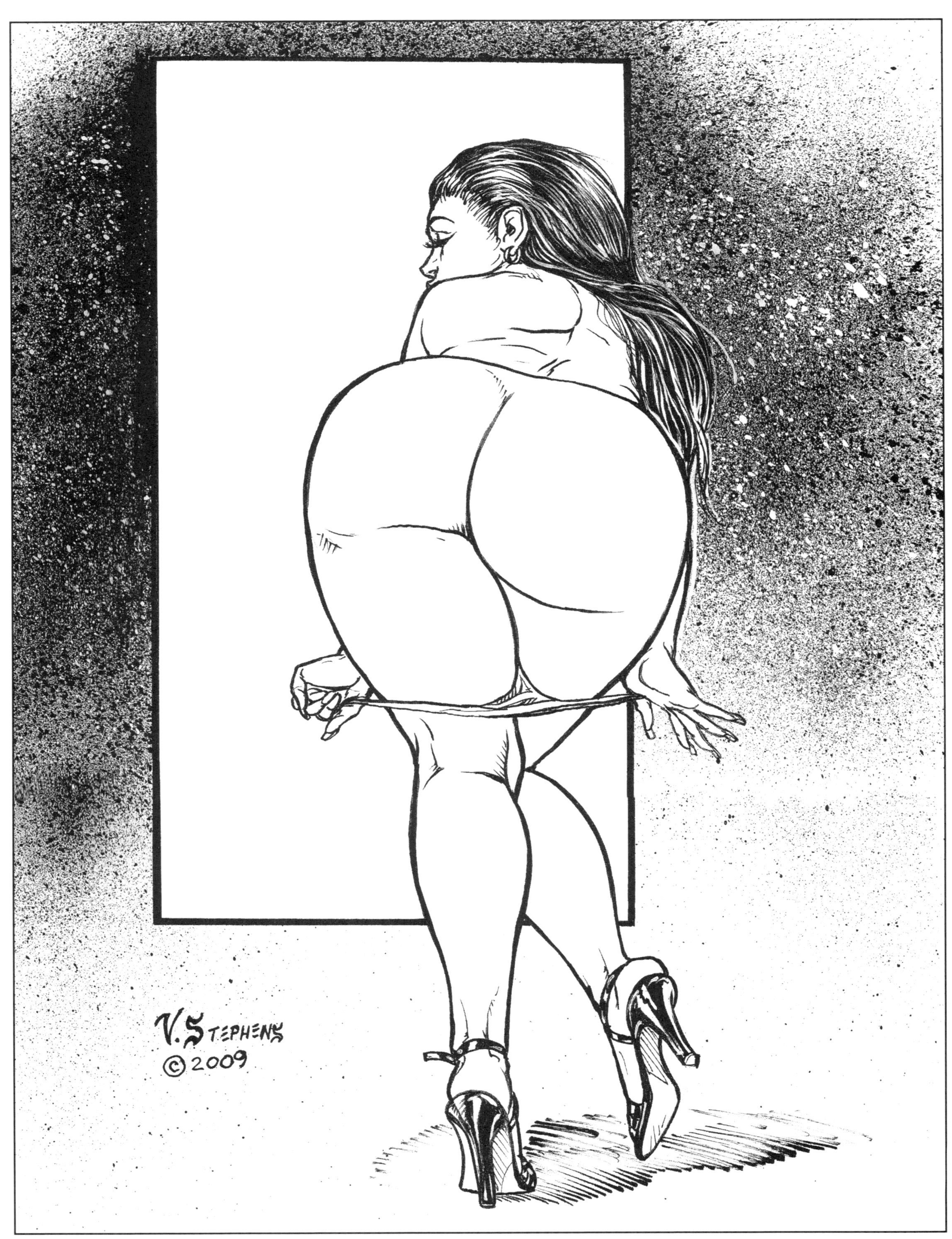
V. STEPHENS
©2009

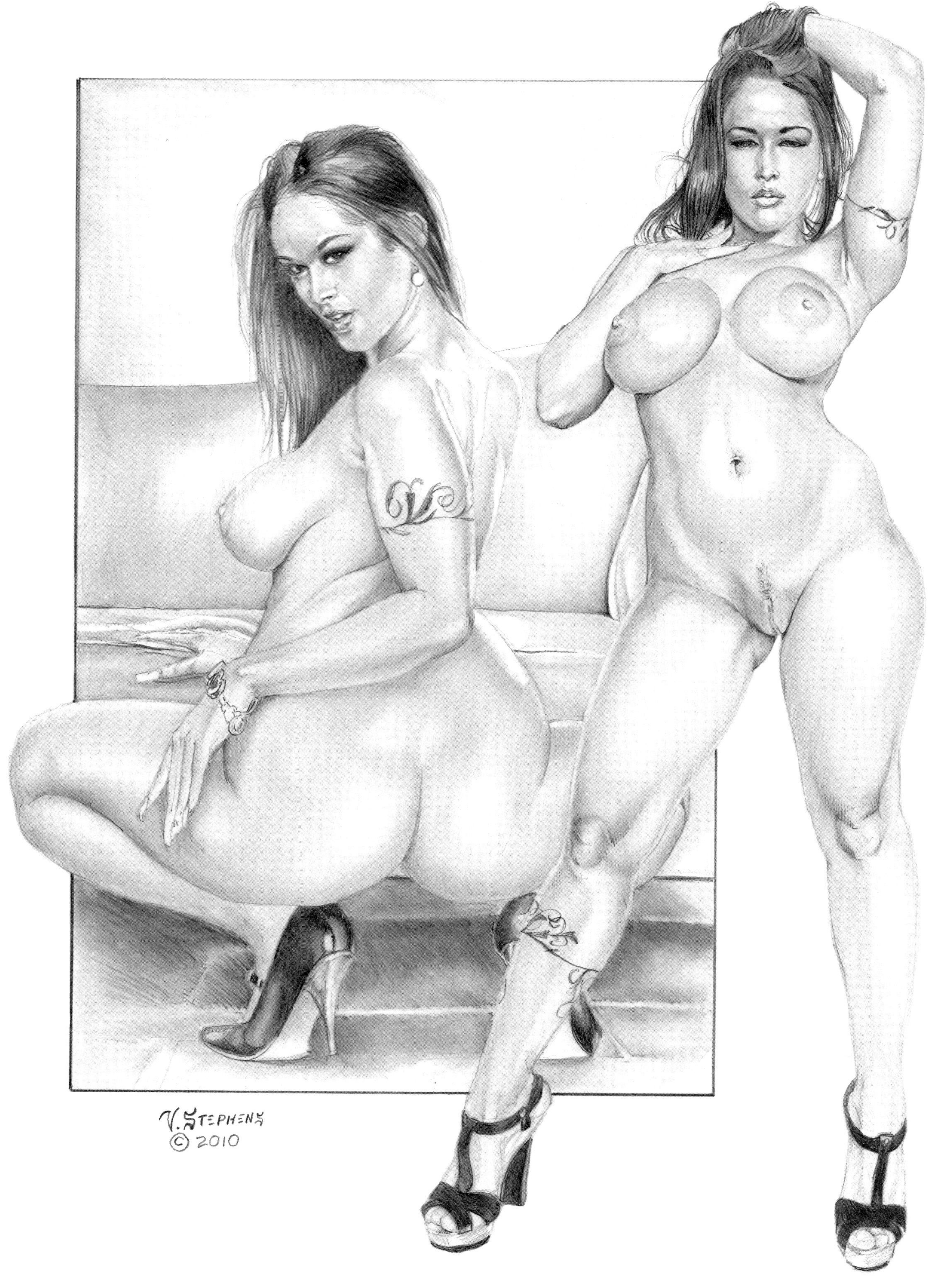
V. STEPHENS
© 2010

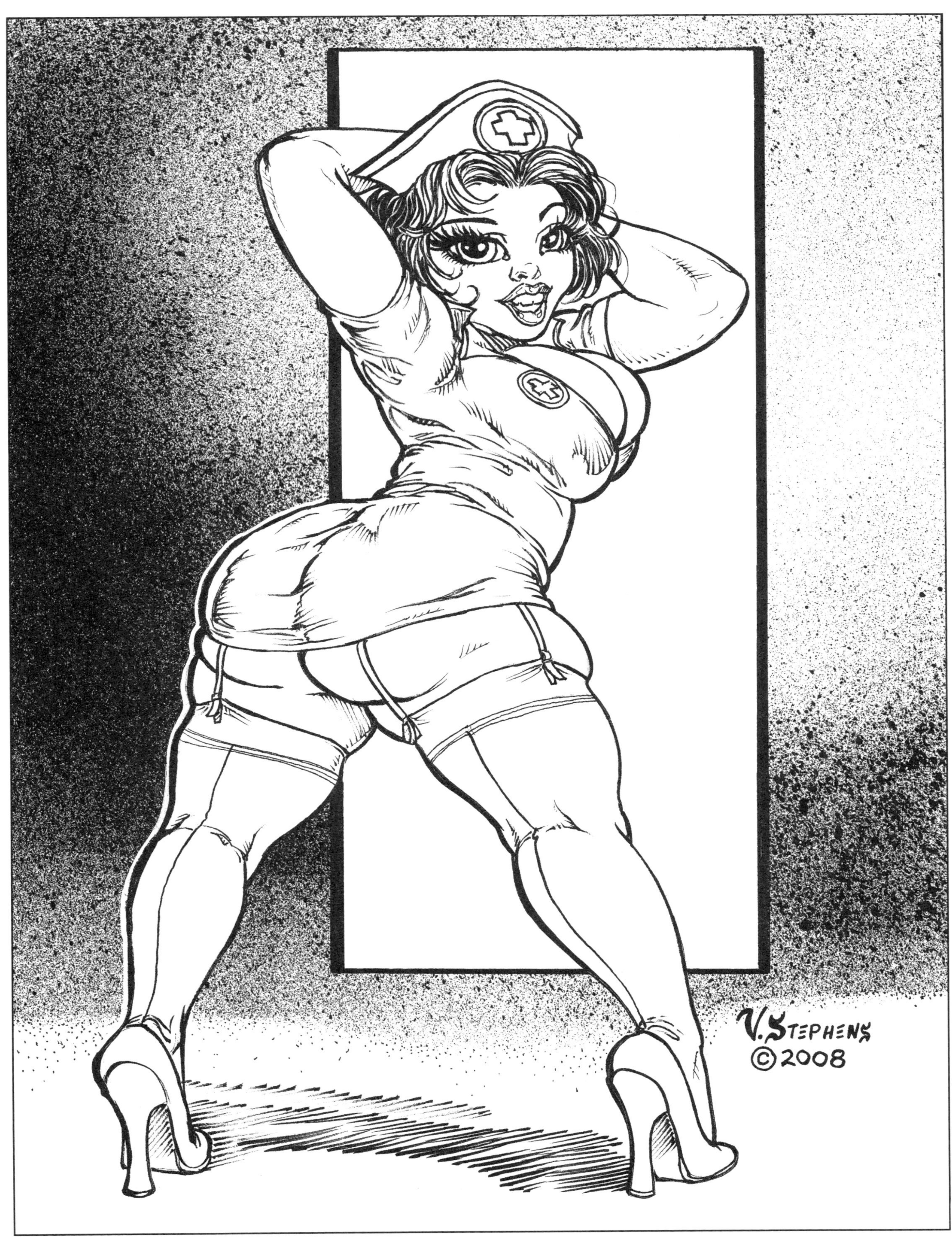
V. STEPHENS
©2008

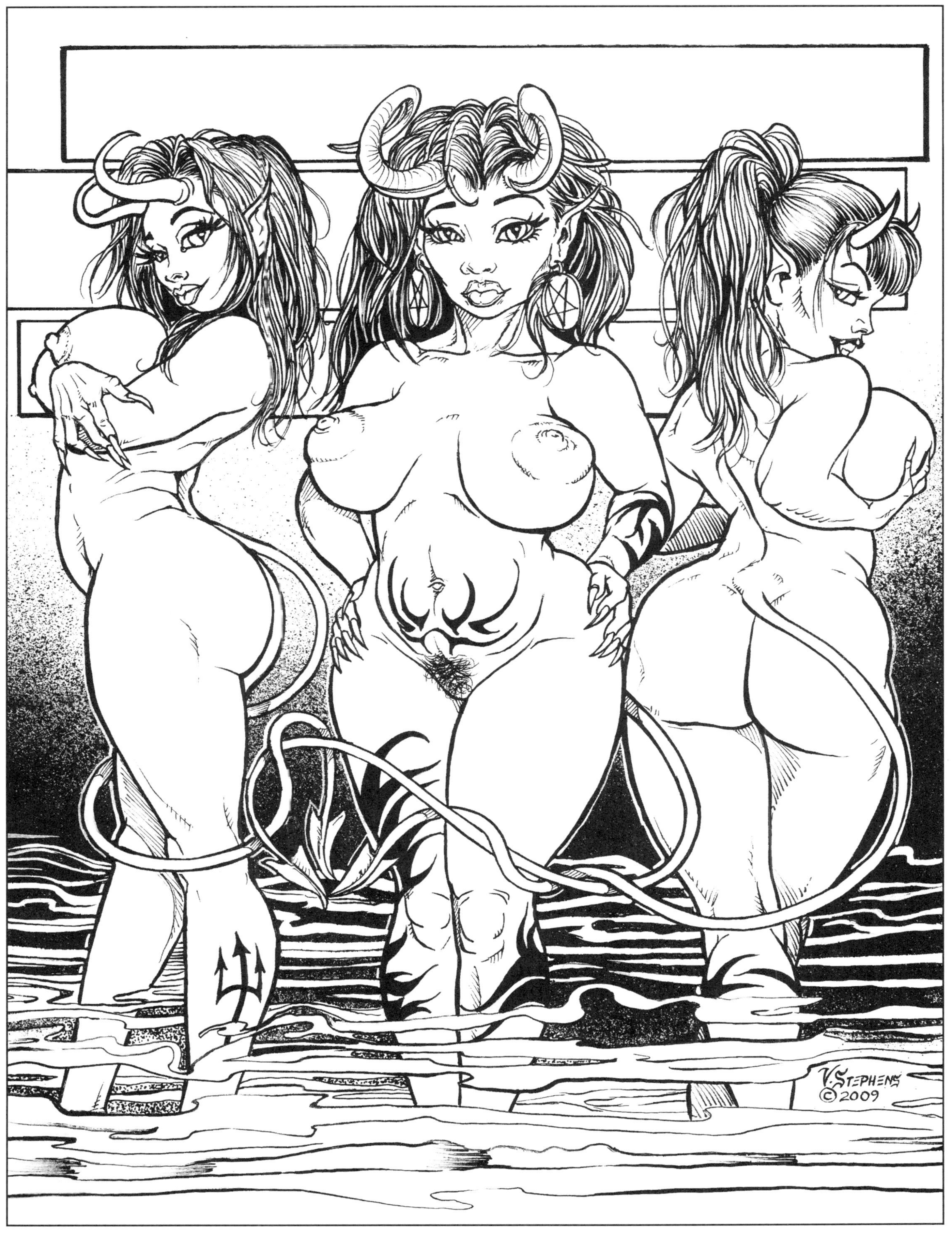
V. STEPHENS
©2009

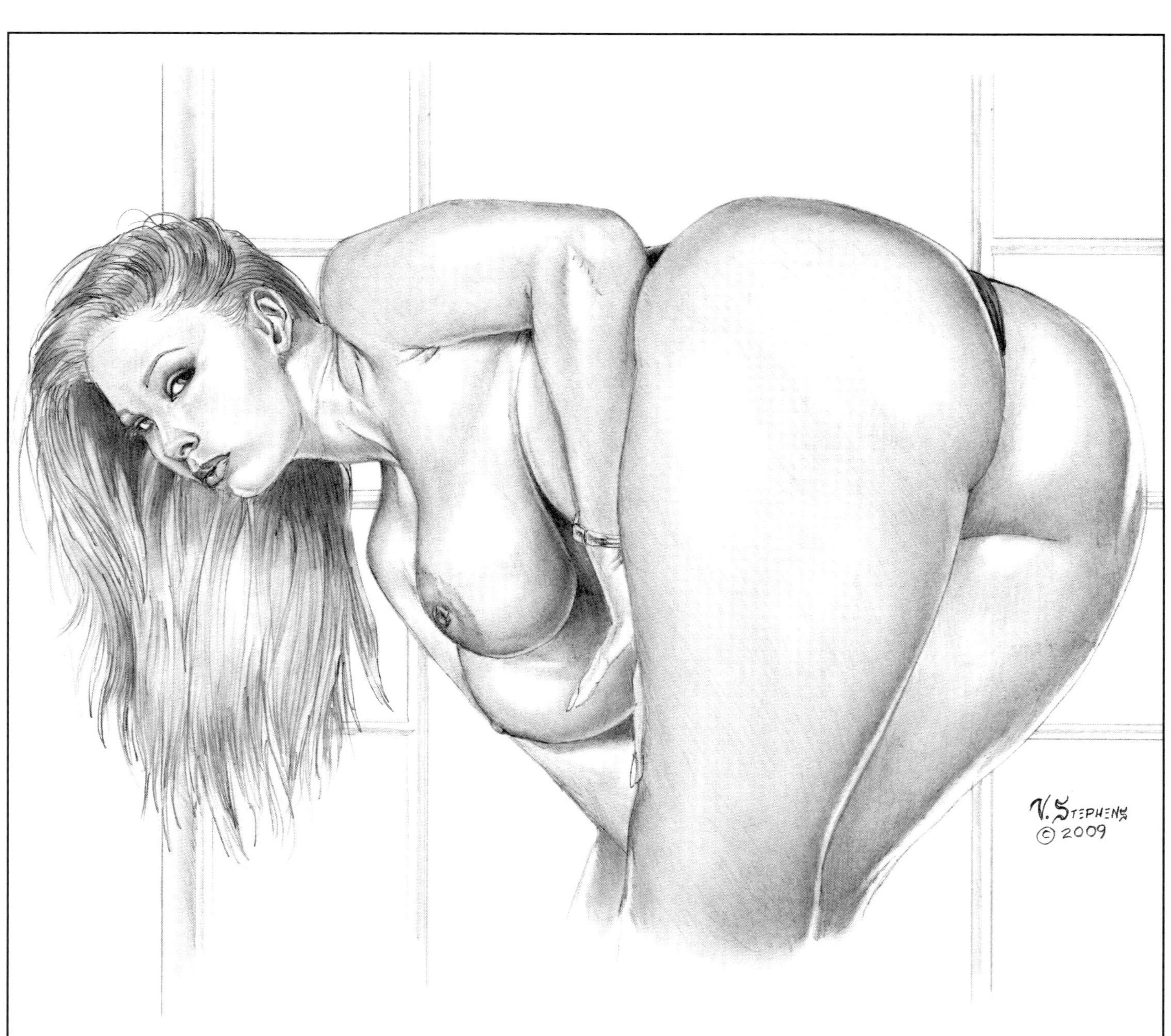
V. Stephens
© 2009

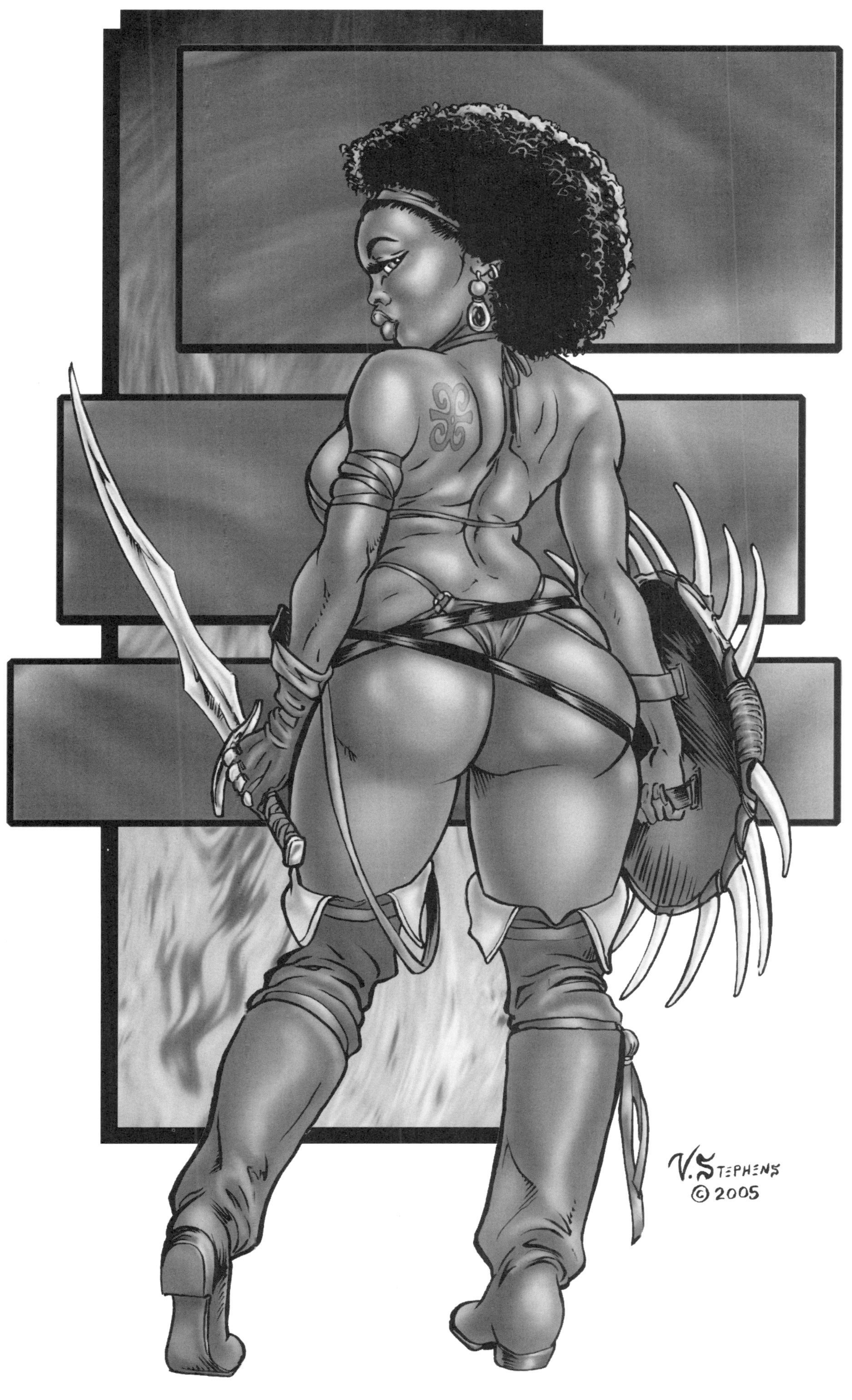
V. STEPHENS
© 2005

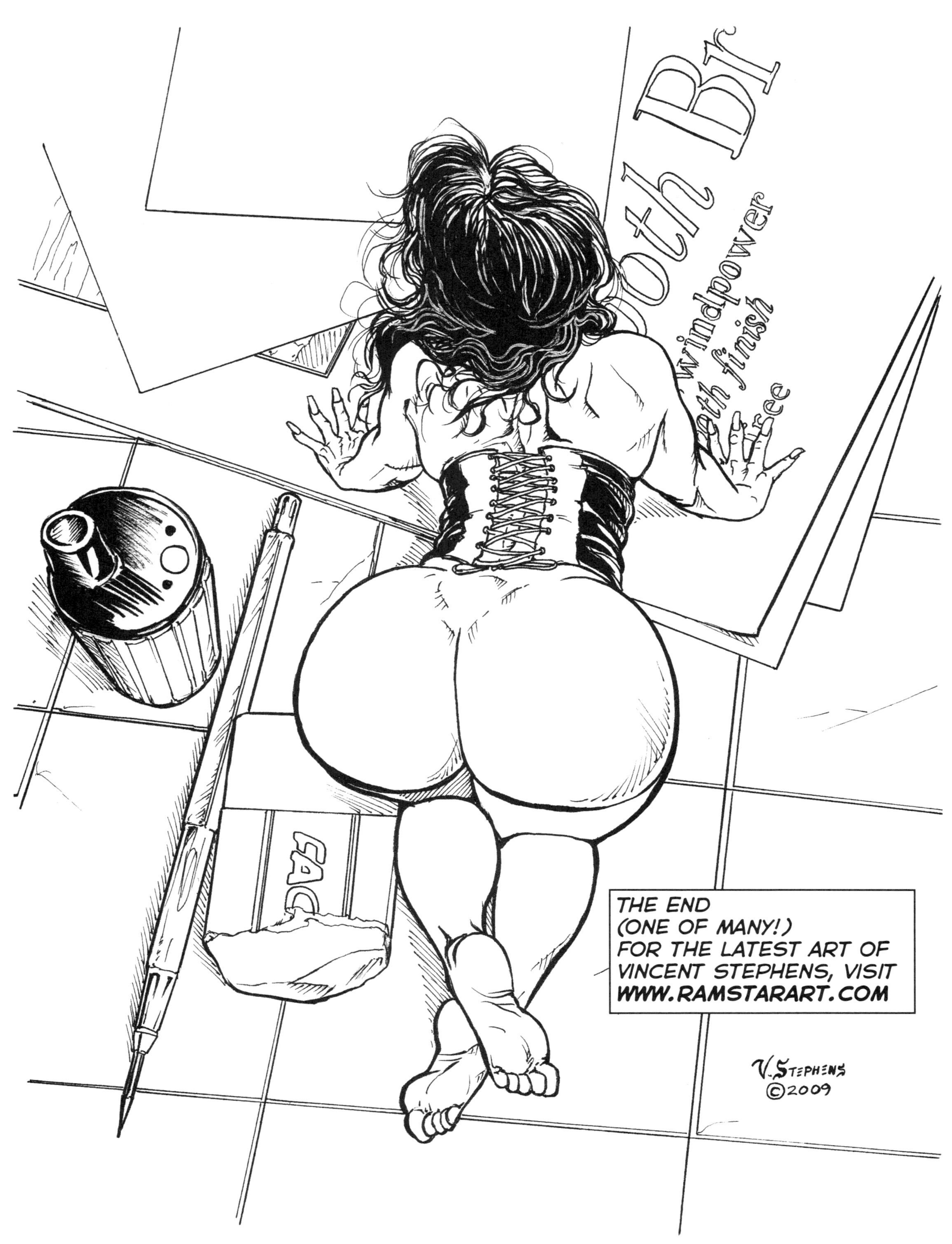
windpower
THE END
(ONE OF MANY!)
FOR THE LATEST ART OF
VINCENT STEPHENS, VISIT
WWW.RAMSTARART.COM
V. STEPHENS
©2009